DORCHESTER PAST

Jo Draper

Phillimore

2001

Published by
PHILLIMORE & CO. LTD.
Shopwyke Manor Barn, Chichester, West Sussex

ISBN 1 86077 175 0

Printed and bound in Great Britain by
BIDDLES LTD.
Guildford, Surrey

Contents

List of Illustrations

Frontispiece: The centre in 1860

Acknowledgements

I am very grateful to Christopher Chaplin for much help with this book; for the index and for the maps nos. 23, 58, 76, 99, 138 and 145. To Peter Bellamy for the maps nos. 8, 12 and 16; to Victoria Palmer for the map no. 35; Wessex Archaeology for the map no. 38; the Duchy of Cornwall for nos: 149 and 150; to all those listed in the picture credits for photographs; and to Sheena Pearce for word-processing it all. The Dorset County Library, both Reference and Lending, has helped throughout with their customary cheerfulness.

Picture Acknowledgements

Richard Baker for nos. 89 and 133; Channons for no. 111; the Dorset County Library for the dust jacket; the Dorset County Museum for frontispiece, nos. 2, 3, 4, 5, 7, 9, 11, 13, 22, 24, 25, 28, 36, 37, 42, 50, 51, 53, 57, 60, 63, 65-67, 70-72, 74, 77-86, 88, 90, 93-95, 98-100, 107, 108, 110, 112, 113, 116, 122, 124, 125, 130, 132, 134-136, 139 and 140; *Dorset Evening Echo* no. 4; Dorset Record Office no. 44; Kathleen Faulkner (née Vidler) nos. 105, 114, 115, 129 and 131; Michael and Polly Legg for no. 87; Marion Makinson for no. 68; Roger Mayne for no. 29; John North for nos. 19, 27, 30, 48 and 148; Bill Putnam for nos. 69 and 104; Royston Tee for Dunford family photographs nos. 61, 62, 144 and 147. Nos. 103, 120 and 121 are from Official Town Guides, and no. 45 is from *Coaching Days and Coaching Ways* (1893) by W. Oatram Tristam.

Any not listed belong to the author, or David Burnett, Dovecote Press.

For Alistair Chisholm,
Dorchester Town Crier

Introduction

Dorchester has been Roman *Durnovaria* and Hardy's 'Casterbridge' and is now growing into the Prince of Wales' Poundbury, a blueprint for the future. But it has always been the market town for a large rural area, and is still an old-fashioned county town. Daniel Defoe visited in the early 18th century and really fell for the place, writing, 'a man that coveted a retreat in this world might as agreeably spend his time, and as well, in Dorchester, as in any town I know in England'. Defoe had seen most of the towns of England, travelling to write his *Tour through the Whole Island of Great Britain* (1724), so his opinion was worth having. Anthony Ettricke defined the town neatly in *Britannia* (1695): 'Upon the river Frome lies Dorchester, a pretty large town, with very wide streets, and delicately situated on a rising ground, opening at the south and west ends, into sweet fields and spacious downs.'

The town they admired had one main street running up the hill (High Street) and another running at right angles to it (South Street). It was enclosed by the Roman banks (later laid out as

1 Looking up Weymouth Road in 1922, with no houses. Dorchester's avenues on the approach roads were as famous as the Walks. The cemetery is on the left.

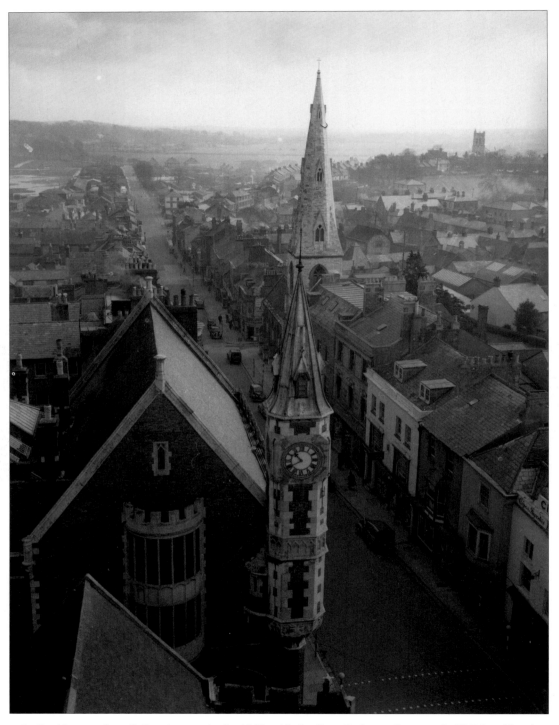

2   Looking east from St Peter's tower in the 1940s with the Corn Exchange foreground, All Saints Church and High East Street behind. Fordington church tower is background right.

3 A wet day in Cornhill in the later 1940s. The street was about to be made one-way, and is now pedestrianised.

walks) with the River Frome running along the north side. The built-up area stopped abruptly on all sides, with open fields beyond. These belonged not to Dorchester but to Fordington, the village which adjoined Dorchester on the east. This unusual pattern of a village actually abutting a town stopped Dorchester growing suburbs until the very late 19th century, when Fordington's open fields were finally enclosed. The middle of the town still preserves its traditional pattern. The buildings are a medley of dates, styles and materials, including timber, stone and several colours of bricks. Thankfully, all the buildings are still on a human scale; the only multi-storey car park is underground.

There is a long and colourful history behind all this. The area has been settled for 6,000 years, and preserves monuments from all periods of history. People have been interested in this history for a long time. The 1695 edition of Camden's *Britannia* gives the late 17th-century view of the Roman town: 'the walls having been pulled down by the enrag'd Danes [i.e. Saxons], who here and there about the town have thrown up several barrows. Yet it dayly discovers some visible foot-steps of Antiquity … some brass and silver coins of the Roman Emperors which the common people call *King Dorn's pence*, whom they fondly conceive, in allusion to the name, to have been the founder of this town'.

4   Dorchester from the north during the floods of December 2000, giving a good view of the abrupt join of town and country along the river, and showing clearly the intricate channels which used to flood the watermeadows.

5   Looking up South Street about 1900, with a large amount of traffic at the other end. The houses above the *Temperance Hotel* (left) were where Hardy worked as an architect's assistant from 1856-62 and where William Barnes had his school from 1847-62.

The enraged Saxons are a nice thought, as is making them responsible for Bronze-Age barrows which pre-date the Saxons by at least a thousand years. King Dorn is a complete invention but he does at least give human interest.

One

Earliest Times

The town of Dorchester is in an area which has been used since the Neolithic period, almost 6,000 years ago. The very earliest people were hunter-gatherers who lived in small groups and had little effect on the landscape. Agriculture arrived in the Neolithic, and fixed settlements came with it. In the Dorchester area there are several large Neolithic monuments, some surviving as earthworks, others invisible until excavation.

Studies of the soils around Dorchester, both on the hills and in the river valley, show that before the Neolithic period the whole area was covered in mixed woodland formed mainly of oak, ash and hazel. Clearance of this woodland led to erosion, just as it has with the clearance of rain forest in South America today. In the Dorchester area the chalk subsoil probably meant that the original woodlands were light and easy to clear, and more useful as grassland after the clearance. Even the valley of the Frome was grassy rather than swampy.

The Neolithic period lasts from about 4200 BC to 2200 BC, two thousand years. The monuments around and in Dorchester were not all in use at the same time, but follow in a sequence. It is impossible to say what most of them were for: ritual or religion seems likely because none of them is defensive or otherwise useful. So many in such a small area is unusual, only found in two or three other parts of the country.

The earliest earthwork in the area is the causewayed camp at Maiden Castle, built about

6 Maiden Castle from the air, showing the huge extent of the hill-fort in its latest phase. The little ripple across the middle shows the ditch of the first hill-fort, which only defended the eastern part of the hilltop. The Neolithic enclosure was on the same line. The elaborate late Iron-Age entrances at each end of the fort show clearly.

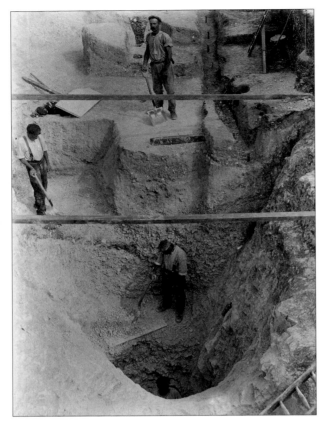

3900 BC and consisting of two ditches and a bank enclosing a roughly circular area. At this time the land north of Maiden Castle was still wooded, so the camp was on the edge of the cleared area. It wasn't a settlement, and it still isn't clear where the people who built it were living. Occasional partially worn-away pits of the same sort of date, such as a couple found at Flagstones, may be parts of settlements the rest of which have been eroded away.

After the causewayed camp had been deserted for perhaps a hundred years, an extraordinary bank barrow was constructed, longer than any other in the country: 546 metres. Originally it was a long thin mound with a ditch either side, built around 3350 BC, at much the same time as a more common type of monument, a long

7 Excavating Maumbury Rings.

8 The Maumbury Rings-Mount Pleasant Ridge, with a remarkable density of early sites. Only Mount Pleasant and Maumbury had surviving earthworks and were known before excavation. The others were revealed by work prior to the bypass and housing development. The site of the two barrows was known from field-name evidence, but their exact location was lost until recent excavations. The smaller ring inside Mount Pleasant is probably a huge building, 38 metres across.

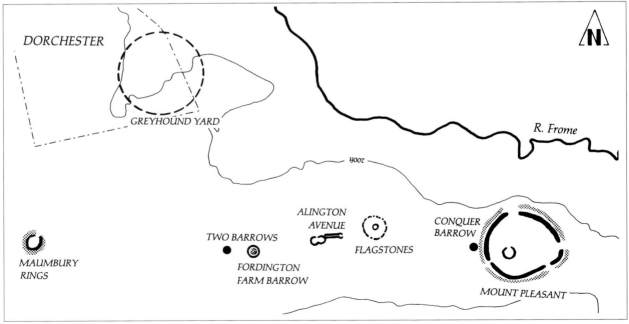

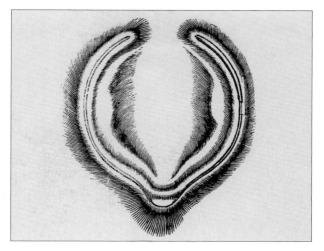

9 The bank at Maumbury after excavation. The clear dark line half-way up the section is the top of the Neolithic bank, and the chalk above it is the Roman addition. The small ditch in the foreground is part of the Civil War alterations.

10 Wood engraving by William Barnes showing Maumbury, 1830s.

barrow, was constructed at Alington. Two more long barrows close to Maiden Castle may be a little bit earlier. Most of these long barrows were clearly used for burial, but the bank barrow has no burials and is perhaps best seen as marking a boundary. Soon after it was built woodland re-grew on the hilltop, suggesting that the area was abandoned.

Close to the Alington Long Barrow at Flagstones was a circular enclosure made out of segments of ditch, about 100 metres across. It dates from about 3300 BC, and on the sides of some of the pits making the ditch patterns had been carved in the solid chalk. Other pit-rings found along the bypass were smaller, but similar. Another has been recently discovered at Dorchester Middle School.

One of the most surprising archaeological finds of recent years in Dorchester was an arc of huge post-holes found in the Greyhound Yard excavations (under Waitrose). Twenty-one were found, close together, forming a small part of a circle. If a full circle was originally built, it would have been 380 metres across, surrounded by posts about a metre across. These posts would have used 500 mature oaks. It dates from around 2750 BC, overlapping in time with another huge timber structure just outside the town, Mount Pleasant, and with Maumbury.

Mount Pleasant is a 12-acre enclosure surrounded by a ditch and bank, inside which was a massive wooden building, all dating from around 2500 BC. About 500 years later the bank was replaced by a huge wooden fence. At the

11 One of the deep Neolithic shafts at Maumbury fully excavated, with one of the deer antlers originally used to dig it placed on the side.

Maumbury is different from all the other archaeological remains around Dorchester. Because it is so close to the town, it has continued to be used. Hardy described it in *The Mayor of Casterbridge* as 'melancholy, impressive, lonely, yet accessible from every part of the town, ... an airy, accessible and sequestered spot for interviews', the banks completely cutting off the views inside 'so that, though close to the turn-pike road, crimes might be perpetrated there unseen at mid-day'. Until the 17th century no-one worried about what the earthwork actually was, but Sir Christopher Wren, travelling to Portland to buy stone for St Paul's Cathedral, identified it as a Roman amphitheatre. William Stukely planned it in 1723, and complained that 'on one side stands the gallows so that all the top is much beaten down with trampling of people to see executions. The vulgar call it *Maumbury*, but have no notion of its purpose, though it is a common walk for the inhabitants, and the parapet at top is a noted place of rendezvous, whence you see the town and wide plains of cornfields all around, much boasted of by the inhabitants for most excellent grain' (odd to think of the suburbs of Dorchester producing good grain).

While Maumbury was usually a lonely place, it was occasionally thronged for public meetings or executions. The most famous death here was not by hanging but by burning. In 1705 Mary Channing, a Dorchester girl, poisoned her elderly husband and was condemned to be burnt to death. She 'pleaded her belly' (was pregnant), so execution was delayed until after her son was born. A contemporary account records 'when fixed to the stake she justified her innocence to the very last, and left the world with a courage seldom found in her sex'. She was only 19 when she was strangled and burnt while 10,000 spectators crammed Maumbury to watch. Probably the most recent controversial use of the area was a Sunday in April 1940 when the British Union of Fascists held a meeting which was heckled by soldiers who tried to overturn the loudspeaker van.

Hardy took a great interest in the excavations of 1908-13, designed to sort out whether the banks were those of a 'sun temple' (a prehistoric enclosure), a Roman amphitheatre or a Civil War Fort. It turned out to be all three, a late Neolithic henge monument which was adapted as a Roman amphitheatre and re-used as a fort in the

same time the local woodlands were cleared, and downland developed. The building at the centre was replaced by stones set in a circle, a sort of tiny Stonehenge. This phase of the site is Bronze Age, showing a continuity not found elsewhere in the area.

We know a little about the life of the people in the Neolithic period. They tamed some wild animals, keeping cows, sheep and pigs. They grew primitive grain, but still hunted wild animals and gathered wild fruits, nuts and plants. The big monuments around Dorchester must have had great significance for those who built and used them because they represent an enormous amount of work. They were probably used for religious ceremonies, perhaps seasonal gatherings of large numbers of people, who traded with one another at the same time.

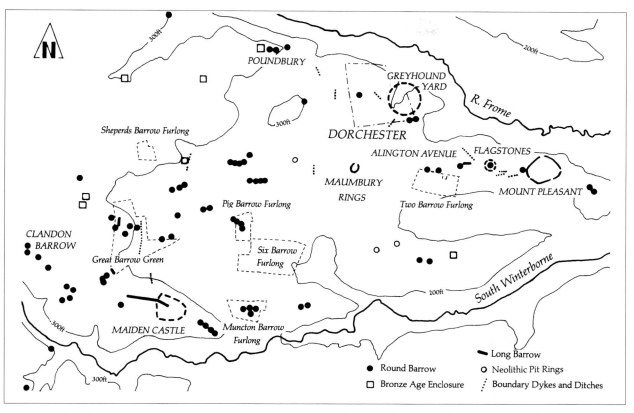

12 The local area in the Neolithic and Bronze Ages, with the outline of the Roman defences showing Dorchester. The Neolithic sites cluster along the ridge to the east (right) of the map, with Mount Pleasant, Flagstones and Alington Avenue close together. The Bronze-Age barrows are very dense, the field names from Fordington tithe map showing those which were destroyed by agriculture. Those close to Maiden Castle (Great Barrow Green) survive because this was pasture. The small pieces of the ditches shown must be parts of a more complete system of Bronze-Age land boundaries.

17th century. The Neolithic monument was a bank with a ditch inside it, and odd shafts (or deep pits), all 32-35 feet deep, cut into the chalk. There were probably 45 of these, but only eight were fully excavated. Some of the antler picks used to dig them out more than 4,500 years ago were found. The purpose of the enclosure and its shafts is still not fully understood, but it must have been ritual or religious.

The Neolithic period was succeeded by the Bronze Age, which is simpler and clearer. In the Dorchester area round burial barrows are the most common feature, and many are still visible today as circular mounds, usually prominently sited. The antiquarian William Stukely described the view south from Maiden Castle in 1720 'for sight of barrows, I believe not to be equalled in the world'.

He was looking at the Ridgeway where the barrows are still remarkably dense. The immediate area of Dorchester has plenty as well, with some inside the later defences of both Poundbury and Maiden Castle, and a large one actually on the bank of Mount Pleasant. There were at least two within the town of Dorchester, presumably levelled by the Romans when the town was laid out. In the 1720s Stukely recorded that 'some farmers were levelling another great barrow; but the people of Fordington rose in arms and prevented them'. Rare early conservationists.

The Neolithic long barrows were used for the burial of a few bones from many people; by contrast the Bronze-Age barrows only have a single (but complete) burial or cremation. This must mark a radical change in society: it seems

13   The huge mound of the largest Bronze-Age barrow in the Dorchester area, the Lanceborough barrow, 130ft. across and 21ft. high. Great Barrow Furlong in Fordington Field was named after it. Camped around, just under Maiden Castle, are the Dorset Yeomanry, looking a little like the invading Roman Army must have done in AD 43. Whilst digging a hole on top of the barrow in 1862 for a new flagstaff, the Volunteers discovered a Roman burial inserted into the old barrow. The photograph is probably 1880s.

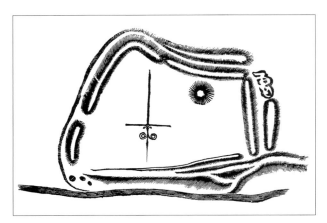

14   Poundbury hill-fort planned by William Barnes in the 1830s. Poundbury was much smaller than Maiden Castle, and had fewer and slighter defences. The mound inside is a Bronze-Age barrow which was there before the fort was built.

that some people were much more important than others. Those buried were presumably the chieftains. Cremations were contained in pots, and some barrows have grave-goods as well. For instance, when the still impressive Clandon Barrow, west of Dorchester, was partly excavated in 1882, a rich burial with grave-goods including gold, jet and amber was found, along with three later burials.

From excavations we know that the people buried in the barrows lived in circular huts, usually grouped together, and sometimes enclosed by a bank and ditch. There was one such settlement on the eastern slopes below Poundbury, which had big boundary ditches that were probably part of a much wider system of land boundaries. Many of the little square fields which showed as earthworks around Dorchester before recent ploughing probably started in the Bronze Age.

15 Faint traces of Iron-Age fields to the north-west of Maiden Castle. They have since been ploughed away, but when this aerial photograph was taken in the 1930s large areas still survived.

The whole pattern of agriculture, settlements and large-scale land divisions is much clearer than it was in the Neolithic period, but apart from Mount Pleasant there is no big occupation site or 'religious' focus as there was earlier.

The smaller settlements of the Iron Age (which starts around 600 BC) follow a similar pattern, and had many little fields. The banks of most of these have been ploughed away, leaving only marks in the soil. Amazingly, we know the name of the local Iron-Age tribe—the Durotriges—because it was recorded by the Romans. The Iron-Age hill-forts near Dorchester are the most spectacular monuments in the area. Poundbury and Maiden Castle both start in the early Iron Age, but Poundbury did not develop. It was re-fortified just before the Roman invasion, and an open settlement outside it, on the hill slopes, continued in use all through the Iron Age.

Presumably Maiden Castle, the most impressive hill-fort in the country, took over the population of Poundbury hill-fort.

Sir Mortimer Wheeler's famous excavations at Maiden Castle in the 1930s were the first in the country to appeal to the public imagination. He discovered the Neolithic phases of the site, and showed that in the Iron Age it developed from a small enclosure with a single bank and ditch, originating around 500 BC. Gradually the hill-fort was enlarged, given complex entrances and additional banks and ditches, reaching its present form around 100 BC. Many people lived inside the fort: it was not just a place of refuge for people and their animals at times of war, as was once thought. Maiden Castle has often been seen as the ancestor of Dorchester, as an Iron-Age defended town, and although there are many differences between

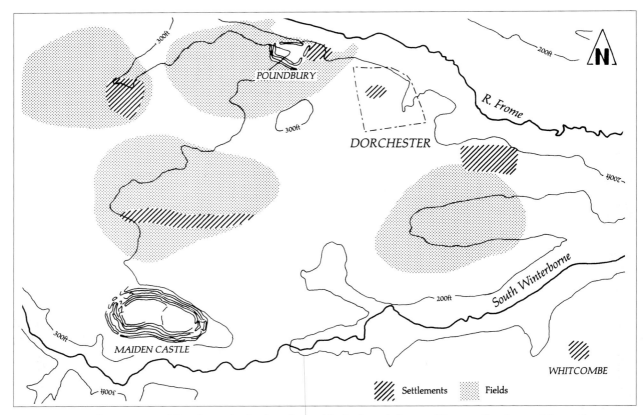

16   The area around Dorchester in the Iron Age, with the later defences of Roman Dorchester. Many of the small fields can still be seen as soil-marks on aerial photographs, and the settlements at Dorchester and Whitcombe must originally have had fields, but they cannot now be distinguished. The Iron-Age settlement at Dorchester is difficult to fix precisely.

17 Two young men killed defending Maiden Castle from the Romans and buried by their surviving comrades. Their legs are entangled. Five pots were buried with them, along with an iron knife and axe, presumably to supply them for their long journey. Many of the War Cemetery burials also had joints of meat buried with them.

18 The spine of one of the Iron-Age defenders of Maiden Castle, with the Roman arrow-head which killed him embedded in the bones. His jaw showed a severe cut from a Roman sword.

towns and hill-forts, it seems a reasonable comparison.

When the Romans invaded Britain in AD 43, Vespasian, one of the Roman generals, was described as taking more than twenty *oppida* in Southern Britain, a word that can be loosely translated as a sort of town. These must have been the hill-forts of southern England and Maiden Castle is the one which has the best evidence of the Roman Conquest. In the eastern entrance Wheeler found the 'War Cemetery', 38 skeletons of the late Iron Age, many of which showed cuts on the bone produced from fighting injuries. Most graphically, one man had an iron arrow-head of Roman type embedded in his spine; a real collision of two cultures. These must be the slain defenders of Maiden Castle, buried by their surviving comrades.

Two

The First Town

Until the Roman invasion of AD 43 there were no towns in the country, unless hill-forts are seen as a primitive sort of predecessor. The area which became the Roman town had already been used for farming, settlement and burial when the Romans started to build. The inhabitants of the town would have been largely the local peoples, not invading Romans. The Romans were good at converting those they conquered into 'civi-lised' citizens.

Dorchester as an urban settlement owes a good deal to the Romans: the town has stayed on the site they chose, and their wall continued to be the boundary of the built-up area until the 19th century. The name itself is derived from the Roman name, *Durnovaria*, which was recorded in a third-century route-book. It used to be assumed that, like most other Roman towns, Dorchester started as a fort for the Roman army after the Conquest. An early Roman army belt buckle has been found in the town, but large-scale excavations over the last forty years have failed to find any trace of a fort, which would have had extensive defensive ditches.

Wherever they are excavated the streets of the Roman town are the earliest features, with only bare earth beneath them. This suggests that they were laid out very early in the life of the

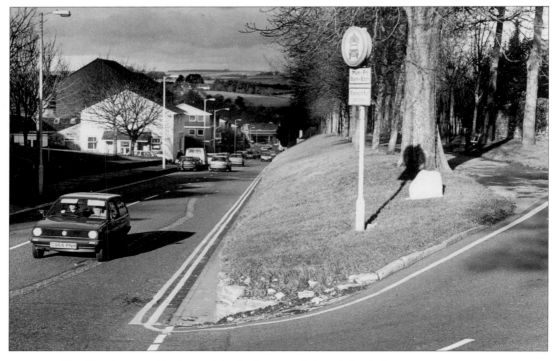

19   The Grove, with the road in the Roman ditch and the defences towering over it.

20   The pitiful remains of the Roman town wall at Top o' Town in the 1930s. All the facing stones have gone leaving just the core.

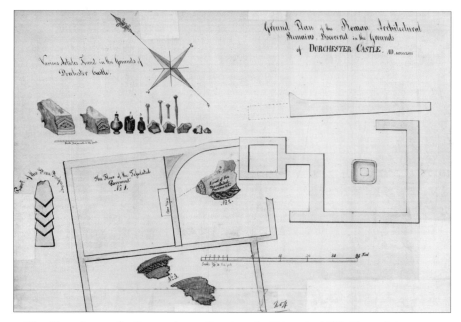

21   Plan of part of a Roman house found at the Prison in 1858. Two of the rooms had mosaic pavements, and large stone tiles from the roof were also found (reconstructed left). A selection of the Roman pottery, painted plaster and bone pins is illustrated, along with two carved stones which are medieval and probably originally came from the Castle.

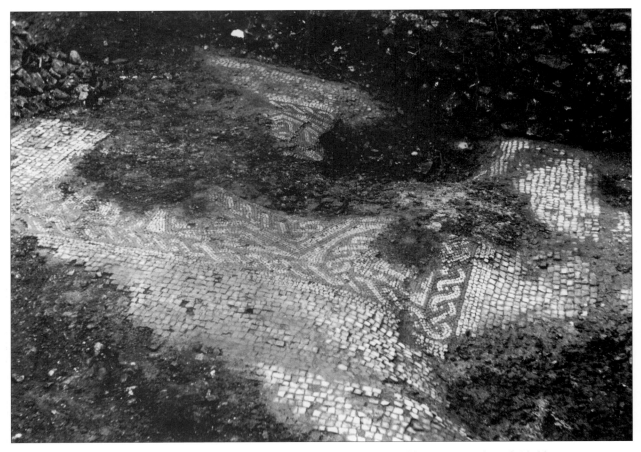

22 Roman mosaic pavement found in Trinity Street in 1905, looking like a carpet. It has subsided because it was laid over earlier pits or post-holes. The twisted border shows well, but the centre has been destroyed.

settlement. The exact date of the foundation is still not clear: timber buildings dating from the AD 60s have been found in several places by excavation, so it seems likely that the town was established soon after the Roman Conquest in AD 43. There were no defences until about AD 150, when a single bank and ditch were constructed. This was heightened in the fourth century, and a stone wall added. These defences formed the town boundary for fifteen hundred years, and are still a clear line. The most impressive remains today are along the Grove, where the road is in the ditch and the bank towers over it. The only blurred part of the defences is along by the river, but excavations here have shown that the ditches continued on this side too.

The layout of many of the streets is known, and it seems likely that the forum or market place was in the centre, around the area of St Peter's church. Large public baths were discovered and excavated in Wollaston Field in the 1980s, but little is known of the other major town buildings like temples. The most complete town house was excavated just before the Second World War in Colliton Park, where remains can still be seen. It is one of the many stone buildings which began to replace the earlier wooden ones from the second century onwards. In plan it is rather unusual for Roman town houses because it is not arranged around a court-yard. The finer rooms, which had mosaic pavements, vary in size from about 12 feet square to 22 feet by 12 feet. Several rooms had

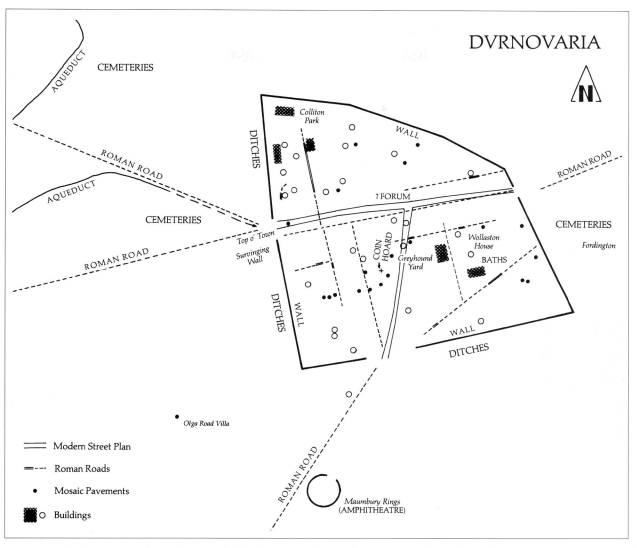

DVRNOVARIA

AQUEDUCT

CEMETERIES

ROMAN ROAD

AQUEDUCT

CEMETERIES

ROMAN ROAD

DITCHES

Colliton Park

WALL

ROMAN ROAD

? FORUM

Top o' Town

Surviving Wall

COIN HOARD

Greyhound Yard

Wollaston House

BATHS

CEMETERIES

Fordington

DITCHES

WALL

WALL

DITCHES

Olga Road Villa

— Modern Street Plan

--- Roman Roads

• Mosaic Pavements

○ Buildings

ROMAN ROAD

Maumbury Rings
(AMPHITHEATRE)

23 Roman Dorchester, *Durnovaria*. Modern excavations and many years of recording finds from the town still give us only a patchy picture of how it must have looked. The street pattern is clearly different from the medieval (and modern) one, although many of the roads into the town follow Roman routes.

hypocausts (suspended floors with heating underneath), and a less well-fitted room had hearths suggesting it was a kitchen. This was close to a 33 feet deep well. The house was not all of one date, but had gradually been added to, ending up with fourteen or fifteen rooms in the fourth century. The current roads into Dorchester from the east, west and south follow the routes of the Roman roads. The gates to the town were probably where the main entrances are now.

The appearance of the Roman town can be partly reconstructed from excavation evidence and comparisons with other Roman sites. Most of the houses would have been single-storey, and plastered outside. The roofs were of big stone tiles or of red baked clay tiles, and many of the external walls were also painted red, but a darker shade. Some houses had verandahs, held up on small stone columns. The streets were straight and well-gravelled. Many of the houses were set

back behind the street line, with gardens and courtyards. The aqueduct probably supplied water under pressure to several public fountains, and in the middle of town there would have been impressive public buildings. Administration and buying and selling would have been important, just as they were to the later town, and Dorchester's nodal position on the Roman road system meant that many travellers would have passed through.

It is difficult to imagine life in the Roman town. Thomas Hardy, writing about the Roman burials found when building his house at Max Gate on the outskirts of the town, wanted to know 'how did the roofs group themselves, what were the gardens like, if any, what social character had the streets, what were the customary noises ... Were the passengers up and down the ways few in number, or did they ever form a busy

24 Mosaic pavement found in Olga Road in 1899, and probably part of a villa rather than a town house because it is some way out of the town. This 40ft. mosaic was lifted and relaid in the Dorset County Museum.

25 The aqueduct, looking north from Poundbury. The clear shelf in the hillside shows where the ditch which carried the water ran.

26   The Roman town house at Colliton Park under excavation in the later 1930s. The footings are clear, and some of the excavated columns have been set up on the right.

throng such as we now see on a market day'? These questions are still unanswerable.

Maumbury, just outside the town, was adapted by the Romans to make an amphitheatre. The Neolithic entrance was re-used and the bank enlarged, and the enclosure was made more oval in shape. This work was probably done by the Roman army around AD 60 for army training, and it was also used for wild beast shows, circuses, and perhaps even gladiators. It continued in use through the life of the Roman town.

Also outside the town are the large burial grounds of the Roman period. Many were discovered in Fordington: 200 in 1747, which were re-interred in the graveyard, and 50 more in 1838–9 when the level of Fordington High Street was lowered. The most interesting find in Fordington was the tombstone now set inside the church, the only one from Roman Dorchester. It is to the

memory of Carinus, a Roman citizen and therefore an important person, and was set up by his children Rufinus, Carina and Arita and his wife Romana.

Fourteen hundred burials, mostly of later Roman date, have been excavated from Poundbury since 1966. Most have few or no grave-goods and are laid out with their heads to the west, suggesting that this was a Christian burial ground. The skeletons from the cemetery give us a good sample of the people of Roman Dorchester, showing that adult males were mostly 5ft. 4in. to 5ft. 8in. and females 5ft. 2in. to 5ft. 5in. The tallest man was 6ft. 1in. The average life expectancy was about 30 years, but this figure masks a great range of ages. If people survived until they were 20, they had a one-in-three chance of living to over 45. A few people in the cemetery were into their 80s. Many children died, especially under two years old.

27 The exposed remains of the Roman town house at Colliton Park, with the new building put over them in the 1990s.

No Roman temples have yet been found within the town, but one is known on Maiden Castle. The history of the hill-fort immediately after the Roman Conquest is not absolutely clear, but certainly by the second century it was deserted, and in the later fourth century a Roman temple was built inside the abandoned earthworks. Part of a marble statue of Bacchus, a bronze plaque with Minerva and a bronze bull with three horns and three female busts on its back all hint at the pagan religions which must have been practised here. A small hoard of four gold coins and a gold ring, all dating to around AD 403, attests to the wealth of at least some of those who worshipped there.

Perhaps the most impressive memorial to the ingenuity of Roman Dorchester is the aqueduct running for 10 miles along the Frome valley from Frampton. It had to be carefully contoured round the side valleys to maintain its height, coming into town at West Gate (Top o' Town). It ran along the north and east sides of the hill-fort at Poundbury, cutting through the defences. The aqueduct was simply a steep open ditch, calculated to bring nearly 25 million gallons a day into the town from a side stream of the Frome. It was dug in the first century and went on in use right through the Roman period. The water would have been used for fountains, sewers, supplies to houses and the public baths. The source would have been carefully chosen and maintained to make sure the water was clean, but it still seems a lot of effort to bring water to the town at only 70 feet higher than the adjacent (if probably dirty) river. The line of much of the aqueduct is still clear, looking like a narrow shelf on the hillside. A 17th-century map labelled it as 'old dry ditch'.

Besides many which are known from the town centre, mosaics have been found in Fordington, just outside the town walls, and at Olga Road, Victoria Park. The latter is much further out of

28 The Roman temple at Maiden Castle being excavated in the 1930s. The walls were of flint, and the plan was a double square, a small one inside a larger.

the Roman town, and was probably a villa rather than a town house. Many mosaics from the town are now in the Dorset County Museum, Dorchester. They vary from simple two-colour square patterns to complex pictures and patterns in eight or nine colours, which must have been very expensive. In their original settings, with the walls and ceilings covered with brightly coloured patterns, they must have been even more sumptuous. Many were sited over big flues through which warm air passed, an effective form of central heating. From the late third century a distinctive Dorchester style of mosaic existed, with similar patterns used for borders.

The end of the Roman town is not clear. In 407 the Roman Army was recalled from Britain to reinforce the defences of the rest of the empire. Britain had been under attack from the Saxons (and the Picts and Scots) since the fourth century, and barbarians were attacking the rest of the Roman empire from the north.

People probably continued to live in Dorchester, but the aqueduct silted up and there were no new buildings. Roman coins stopped

coming into the country and in the fifth century pottery manufacture ceased, so it is difficult to date any occupation. The Roman town house at Colliton Park had a strange end: many of the columns which had supported its verandah were thrown down the well. It seems stupid to destroy a clean water supply this way, even if the columns were no longer useful.

The popular view of the end of Roman Britain, with the Romans all leaving and the Saxons immediately looting their way across the landscape, is wrong. Only the soldiers left: after 400 years of Romanisation all the people of Britain were Romans. The Saxons did not invade Dorset until perhaps AD 650, and the gap between the Roman soldiers going and the Saxons arriving is so little understood that it used to be called the Dark Ages. Roman forms of government probably survived in Dorchester, and of course agriculture continued, or the people would have starved. The earliest Anglo-Saxon burials found around the town are small groups of seventh-century date, and certainly the Saxons must have taken over the area in that century.

Three

The Medieval Town

We know very little about Dorchester and the area around in the early Saxon period. Archaeology has revealed nothing, and the fact that the medieval (and thereby current) streets are on a different line from the Roman ones suggests that the town was deserted and resettled. The first document to mention the town comes in 789, when the king's reeve (the head man or king's deputy) of Dorchester was killed on the coast by Vikings. Dorchester must have been a considerable size by then to have had such an important official. The town was by this time called *Dornwecestre*, retaining part of its Roman name, *Durnovaria*. Dorset as a shire (or county) was formed by 800, taking its name from Dorchester. The town would have been the centre for courts

29 Vikings from the 1989 Dorchester Community Play *Under the God* (by Ann Jellicoe). The Vikings are confronting the Kings' Reeve from Dorchester. (Photograph by Roger Mayne.)

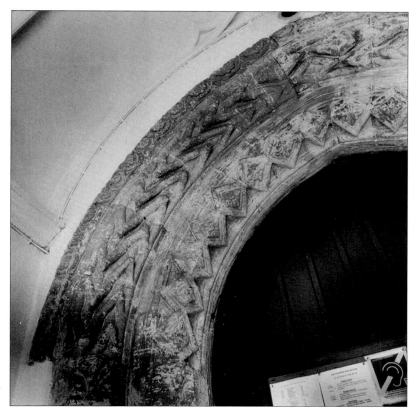

30 The typical zig-zag pattern from the Norman doorway reset when St Peter's church was rebuilt in the 15th century. The rest of the early medieval church was demolished. This is the earliest stonework in Dorchester apart from the remnants of the Roman town wall.

from the late Saxon period, with the system of king's judges and locally recruited juries starting then.

Fordington is also a Saxon settlement. It had extensive Roman cemeteries, and Christian churches were often built in Roman cemeteries because some of the graves were those of Christian martyrs. When St George's church, Fordington was restored early in the 20th century the footings of a smaller church were found beneath it. It was then claimed as Roman, which is very unlikely, but it may well have been Saxon. The church is well sited, in a high position, and it may be that St George's is the earliest church in the area. Because charters are dated from there, we know that Saxon kings had a house in the Dorchester area from the ninth century and it is possible that this was at Fordington, although if so it is difficult to see why Fordington did not develop as the more important settlement.

The Domesday (1086) description of the town (by then called *Dorecestre*) shows that in 1066 there were 172 houses, containing a population of perhaps five to six hundred. As was usual with towns of any size, there were two moneyers making coins. Although only one medieval building survives in the town, present-day Dorchester has grown from the medieval settlement. The main street pattern, the three parishes and their churches are all late Saxon in origin. The only surviving medieval building is St Peter's church; the other two parish churches (Trinity and All Saints) had medieval predecessors, but have been replaced by 19th-century buildings. The plots on which the medieval houses stood were arranged in the same way as the modern plots in the town centre. Long and thin with only a narrow street frontage, the houses were probably partly stone and partly timber, with thatched roofs. Stone and flint would have been easily available from the rubble of the Roman buildings of the town.

Although the main reason for the existence of the town (and one of the major factors making

it a town) was its market, agriculture was still important to medieval Dorchester. The town was limited to the area inside the Roman walls, but there were fields inside all through the medieval period. East and West Walls were the names given to the fields, and they were run as open fields until 1596 when they were enclosed.

Water mills were the only mechanical source of power. There was only one mill actually in the town (Friary Mill) with two more just on the

31 The Norman tympanum at St George's Fordington, showing St George intervening in the First Crusade (on the right side, of course) at the battle of Antioch in 1098, only perhaps ten years before this was sculpted. St George as a knight on a horse with a long banner streaming behind him from his lance is in the centre, with two kneeling crusaders on the left, and on the right are the Saracens St George is overwhelming, one lying dead along the bottom and another being impaled.

32 St Peter's Church, right in the centre of the town, and the only surviving medieval building. Most of the building, including the handsome tower, dates from the 15th century. In 1421 Robert Grenlefe of Dorchester left 20 marks (about £13) for 'the new construction of the body of the church of St Peter'. This was drawn in 1794 by a tourist on his way to Weymouth, who has made the tower shorter than it really is.

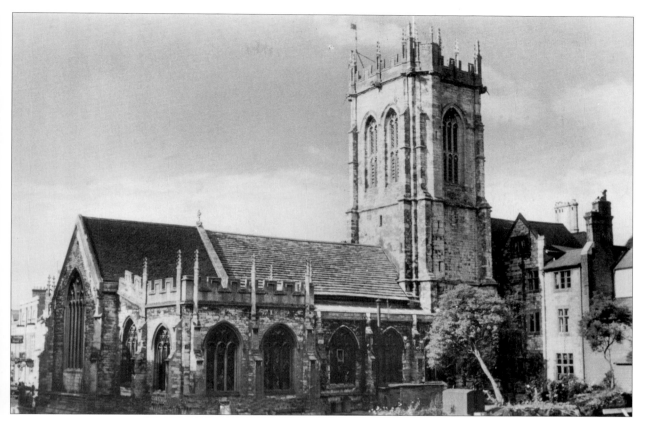

33 A very rare view of the back of St Peter's Church, taken in 1960 when Georgian houses in North Square were demolished. They were replaced by a garage.

outskirts, West Mill and Fordington Mill. These were corn mills, but Loud's Mill, further downstream, was built in the 1590s specifically as a fulling mill for pounding cloth to make it thick and felty. An early 17th-century map shows the tentering racks close by, where the cloth was stretched after fulling.

The main streets would have been lined with houses, some of them with workshops where goods were also sold. There were stalls in the streets: the fish shambles (or market) was on the north side of one of the High Streets, the glovers' stalls in South Street, and the butchers in North Square. The main market area was in the middle of town beside St Peter's church. This is a classic position, right at the junction of the three main streets. Dorchester had many craftsmen, and also merchants. Forty-two Dorchester merchants are listed in a taxation of the 1330s, and although there were twice that number paying in Bridport

and Shaftesbury, the Dorchester tax-payers were much richer.

The three parish churches would have looked very different, all three originally having been plainer buildings, probably with simple square towers. Inside all had several altars, most of them part of a chantry chapel where masses for the dead were said. Some of these were established for individuals or families, but many were set up by the craft guilds of the town for their members. The churches would have been full of bright colour, with painted screens and statues, wall paintings, stained glass and so on.

There were also chapels in the town which have completely disappeared. St Rowald's in South Street was described as out of use in 1420, and little is known besides its position. The Hospital of St John was in the area of Colliton Park, but its exact site is lost. This was founded in the 13th century and, in common with all

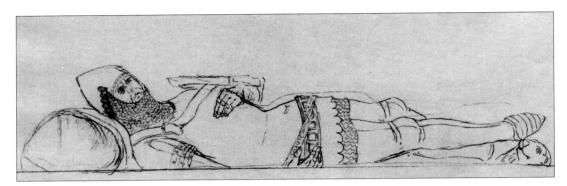

34 Late 14th-century effigies of knights from St Peter's Church. We have lost their names, but they must have been from the town and are the only representations of medieval people from Dorchester. They were drawn in the 18th century.

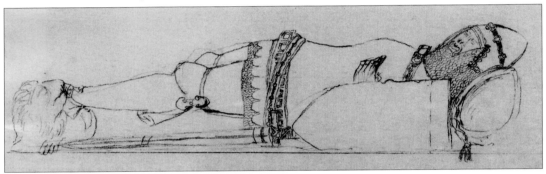

medieval hospitals, was as much for the housing of travellers as for the care of the sick. It was dissolved in 1540, at the Reformation.

A few 14th-century wills survive from Dorchester, and they show the piety of the people. Many left money to Salisbury Cathedral, to their parish church (or even to all three churches), their rector and to the Friary. Most left money also to a chantry in one of the churches so that masses would be said for them after death. In a few extreme cases, virtually all their money was left to establish a chantry: a large landowner, John Syward, who died in 1399 asked his executors to sell all his houses (including one in Southampton) and use the money 'for the benefit of my soul and that of my father, my mother, my family and our benefactors', i.e. to found a chantry.

Dorchester had a castle from soon after the Norman Conquest, built (as many were) actually within the Saxon town, partly as a symbol of the Conquest and partly a refuge for soldiers if there was trouble. It certainly existed well before 1137, when it was enlarged. King John stayed in Dorchester Castle 11 times between 1201 and 1214 on his regular journeyings around the country. These journeys were partly for business and partly for hunting. Payments for the chaplain, falconer, keepers of hounds, carriage of goods, and for horses, occur throughout John's reign, and on one occasion the carriage of wines from Southampton to Dorchester. Repairs name the pigeon house and its chapel as well as the main castle buildings. No repairs are recorded after 1272, and the castle must have gone out of use soon afterwards. This happened to many castles in the 14th century; they were no longer needed because the country was more stable.

The site of the castle is clear on Hutchins 1772 plan of Dorchester, and parts of the castle ditches have been excavated. The footings of an aisled hall found inside the Prison in the 19th century must be part of the castle buildings. The site was given to the Friary in the mid-13th century, who took the stone of the castle buildings for their new Friary just downriver. Most medieval monastic houses were in the countryside but

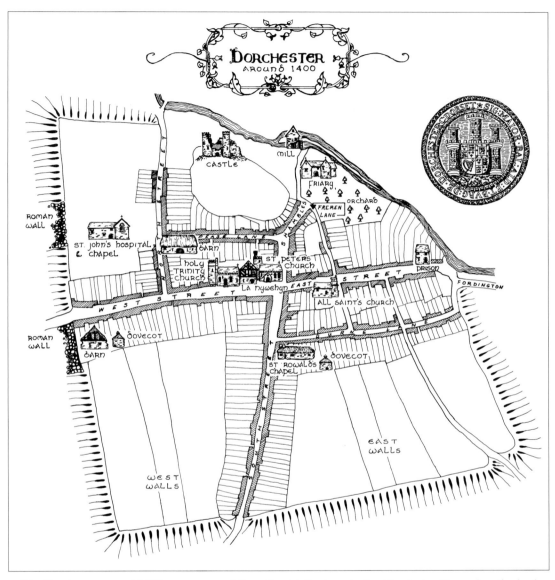

35 Dorchester around 1400, reconstructed from the details given in the Dorchester Domesday, the land registry set up by the Borough in 1395. The exact position of St John's Hospital is not certain but it was in Colliton Park. The little lane beside All Saints Church was called All Hallows Church Lane. The Borough Arms are from the seal of about 1300. (Map by Victoria Palmer.)

friaries were deliberately set inside towns. By 1296 there were 32 friars. Little is known of their buildings, parts of which were converted to a house when friaries were abolished in 1538.

The best portrait of medieval Dorchester is provided by the bye-laws of 1414, a curious mixture of rules about appointing local administrators and hygiene. They illustrate the half-agricultural, half-manufacturing life of the town: no skinner was to beat skins or hides in the street where human food was sold; manure was not to be left in the street for more than a week; pig keepers were to keep their charges under control; and carcasses of animals who died

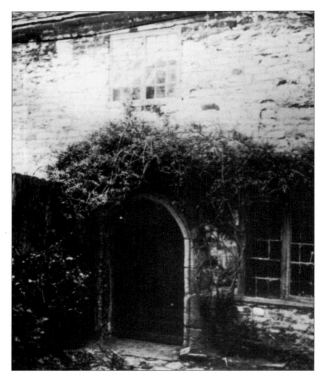

36 This simple late-medieval arch survived in a small building in Colliton Street until 1931 when Thurmans took over the building as a store. The arch was moved to their other shop in South Street where it can still be seen.

were to be dumped out of the town. No baker of white bread (a very superior commodity in the Middle Ages) was to bake barley bread or masline (bread made from mixed wheat and rye, the usual medieval bread). There were three fairs each year, at Holy Trinity (eight weeks after Easter), St John the Baptist (24 June) and St James (25 July), all close together in the year. Another at Candlemass (February) was added in Elizabeth's reign. The three weekly markets were Wednesdays, Fridays and Sundays. The little medieval fields in East and West Walls were open for everyone to graze their cattle from 8 September to 11 November, and on to 2 February for sheep. From February to September the animals were kept off so that hay or other crops could be grown. Fifteenth-century wills mentioning land in East and West Walls call them arable, so crops must have been grown in the strips even though the fields were so tiny.

After they were enclosed in 1596 they became little pasture closes and were gradually overtaken by development.

The bye-laws also set up an early land registry, recording all land transactions in the Borough. It cost 6d. for the use of the town seal, and the clerk was paid 3d. for each entry. This book, called 'Domesday', still survives and most of the information about the geography of medieval Dorchester comes from it. The town was governed by 24 'lawful men' or burgesses who were the equivalent of town councillors, and they elected two bailiffs who were virtually mayors. They employed two constables to keep order in the town, and a clerk to record the meetings. Prudently they decided that 'the Common Chest shall have three different locks, the keys to be kept by three men chosen for the purpose, who shall be changed each year'.

Fordington, despite its proximity to the town, was a classic open field village, with the farmhouses and cottages all actually in the village, some around the green with the church, a pound for straying animals, and the court house where the manor court was held. One mill was in the village, and another further upstream at the hamlet of West Mills. Most open field systems were enclosed from the 17th century onwards, and virtually all were gone by the 19th century. Fordington was an exception; it was not enclosed until 1874.

The arable area, the Great Field, covered 3,000 acres. There were no fences, even between the arable and grazing areas along the meadows. By the time Henry Moule described the farming in the 19th century, the system of dividing the arable into three parts and having one crop (or a fallow) on each had broken down a little. Most farmers in one field would agree as to which crop would be planted, but others would grow something else. This communal cropping had been more uniform in medieval times, and was needed because the farms were not compact blocks, but strips scattered all over the fields.

Grazing was also communal. Even in the 19th century there was a cowherd, who looked after all the cows which grazed on Fordington Moor (Cow Common on the 1779 map) or on Poundbury. East Ward was laid out as water meadows in the 17th century, but was still owned in different strips. It was used for spring grazing by sheep, which right was let by auction and the money used to maintain the complex system of waterways

37 Looking across Fordington Field with Dorchester centre background. This was painted in the late 19th century, but would have looked very much the same in medieval times. The stooked corn is being loaded onto the cart to go back to barns in Fordington.

needed for water meadows. The hayward later marked out the different owners' lands so that they could each make and carry their own hay.

More documents survive from medieval Fordington than from Dorchester, so the picture we have is more complete. A dispute in 1328 shows the sort of powers the vicar of Fordington had then, and how at least some of his parishioners thought he was taking more than his due, both in fees and in the fields. Only the verdict survives: 'he does not fine parishioners for fornication the sum of forty pennies. Nor is it his custom to force the lord's tenants to pay a wedding fee of nine pennies, when from time immemorial the wedding fee has only been threepence. Also he has not been in the habit of coming into Fordington Field with Robert Fode, his house servant and therefrom carrying off peas and beans from the field of the lord and his tenants nor does he allow his swine to wander into the field where he has no common rights. Nor has he received corn carried off by his said servant from the field of the lord and his tenants as he is charged with doing by the whole homage.' The whole homage means *all* the tenants of Fordington; the vicar must have really annoyed the village to get everyone united against him.

A great many of the court records for Fordington survive and they show that, in October and November 1348, 40 tenants died and only four of these had living heirs. In 1607 there were only 71 tenants for the whole of Fordington; there may have been a few more in 1348, but it seems very likely that half the tenants were killed by the Black Death, a graphic demonstration of the huge numbers who died.

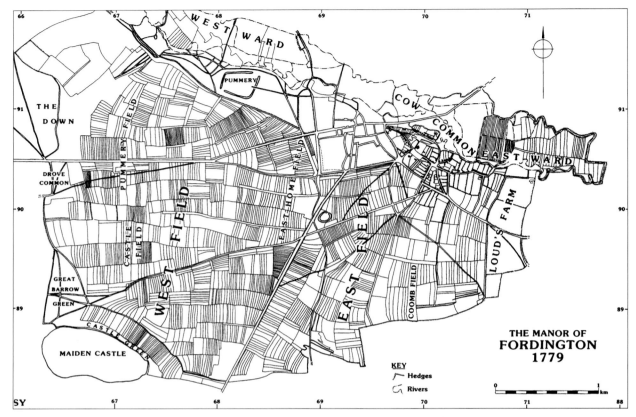

38 Medieval farming survived at Fordington until the late 19th century. Here are the open fields of Fordington as surveyed by Simpson in 1779. The grazing is mostly along the river valley, on the north of the map, but East Ward is divided into strips despite being water-meadow. The small closes in the village were held by individual farmers, but the Great Field, the whole of the arable area, was worked as an open field. (Drawing prepared from the original map by Wessex Archaeology for English Heritage.)

Much detail is known of the parish life in Fordington in the early 15th century because the Register of the Dean's Visits of Inspections survives for 1404-17. Amongst church business in 1405 are noted: timberwork of the rood loft defective, churchwardens to repair; Henry Webb, who had had 16 ewes grazing in the parish and had not paid tithe on their lambs, etc.; also noted are two sets of people accused of adultery, and a husband who had deserted his wife. Those cases were proved. Denise Stury 'accused Agnes Knoll of defaming her among good and serious people of adultery with John, Agnes's husband, so that her reputation was greatly harmed'. Agnes was found guilty and sentenced to 'be beaten thrice in front of procession through church'. Denise and John were again accused at the court in 1408, and at the same time Denise was accused of adultery with the vicar, which she denied, but the Dean ordered her 'to purge with eight hands' (that is, to bring seven witnesses) and ordered the vicar not to meet her in suspect places or receive her in his house on pain of a fine of £10. Katherine Dene was accused of adultery with a friar from Dorchester and at the 1412 court another Fordington woman, Amice Kete, was accused of leaving her husband and keeping a brothel. Half the accusations at every court were for sexual irregularities, and whilst some may simply have been spiteful, surely not all of them were.

Four

Fires, Puritans and Revolt

We know much more about the town from the 16th century because many more documents survive, and a more human picture emerges. The century started with the town at a low ebb and only about 260 houses. In 1535 the townsfolk complained that it was 'outrageously decayed'. This was true of most towns at that time; the country was generally under-populated and London was growing enormously, pulling its population from the rest of the country. In the middle of the 16th century the population of Dorchester was probably only about 1,000 but, despite outbreaks of plague in 1563 and 1579, this had increased to 2,500 or thereabouts by 1642. Such a rise is typical of the period, and was partly due to simple population growth and partly to the expansion of

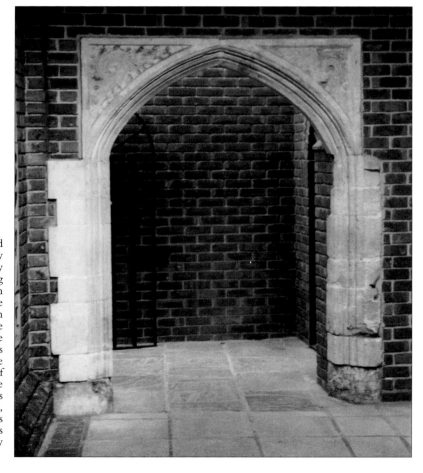

39 The Greyhound Yard arch, dating from the early 16th century, and originally the entrance to a building set longways off South Street. This later became the *Greyhound Inn*. South Street was set back to give wider pavements in the 1890s, and the arch was rebuilt further from the street. When the arcade of shops was built in the late 1950s the arch was reset as the entrance to the car park, and in the 1980s it was moved yet again to its current position by Waitrose.

40   Three figures by Elizabeth Frink, on the site of the Dorchester gallows in the 16th and 17th centuries. These Dorset Martyrs commemorate those who were executed here because of their religious beliefs.

41   The Old Grammar School drawn in 1828, still with the foundation stone of 1569, but as virtually rebuilt in 1618 (it had been damaged in the great fire of 1613). It was heavily restored in 1830 and demolished in 1882. Napper's Mite almshouse on the left was built in 1616 with an open loggia along the front. The street frontage was rebuilt in 1842, but the little courtyard behind still survives.

towns at the expense of the countryside. The town gradually grew, but its physical development was punctuated by fires, whose effects were widespread because so much of it was thatched. *Fire from Heaven*, a contemporary pamphlet describing the fire of 1613, gives a picture of the town before the catastrophe: 'Dorchester is one of the principall places of traffick for westerne merchantes, by which means it grew rich and populous, beautified with many stately buildings and faire streetes, flourishing with all sorts of tradesmen and artificers.'

The biggest change in the 16th century was the Reformation, when all the religious houses and chantries were abolished. Official religion changed from Catholic to Protestant. The monasteries, the Friary and the chantries owned many houses and a little land in Dorchester, and some local people did well from the forced sales. John Churchill, a clothier, bought the lands of the Hospital of St John, and built the first Colliton House on its site. The Churchills moved from

42 Looking up High West Street from Cornhill in about 1800, the new Shire Hall of 1797 can be seen centre. It has been suggested that this painting is a later fake, but details suggest that it is real: the smoothing of the corner about the shop-front shows on later 19th-century photographs, and the buildings sketched in front of St Peter's Church did indeed survive until about 1800. Hutchins in 1774 said there were 'Flemish buildings of plaister' in Cornhill and around St Peter's Church which contrasted with the regular brick and stone buildings in the rest of the town.

being town merchants to country gentry, like the Williams family who had bought Herringston a little earlier. The Grammar School was founded in the late 16th century to replace the schooling earlier provided by the Friary. It stayed on its original site in South Street until the 1920s. Hutchins, the county historian, was educated here in the 18th century. It developed into Hardye's School, and is now united with the girl's secondary school. Trinity School was founded in 1625 in Trinity churchyard, and was merged with the Grammar School in 1883.

In the early 17th century Dorchester was a Puritan centre, largely because of John White, rector of St Peter's from 1606 to 1648. He was called the Patriarch of Dorchester, and promoted emigration to America. In 1630 settlers from Dorchester founded a town of the same name in Massachusetts, which quickly became the largest town in New England (it is now part of Boston). The American settlements were intended to be run on proper Puritan principles, but in theory the emigrants also set out intending to convert the Red Indians.

The bad fire in 1613 was caused by 'a Tallow Chandler there dwelling making too great a fire under his kettle' so that his workshop caught fire. The wind was blowing strongly, and the timber-framed houses were dry because the weather had been hot, so the fire spread quickly. The county's 40 barrels of gunpowder were stored in Shire Hall, close to the outbreak, and it was feared that 'one blast' would blow up the whole town. Bravely, local folk wrapped the barrels in wet sheets and rolled them into the fields, saving the town from explosion. However, 'man, woman

43 The Oak Room at the *Antelope* was two rooms in the 17th century: the panelling and fireplace surrounds date from around 1600 although it has been re-arranged to make room for the Georgian windows. The stone fireplace is a little earlier.

and childe ran amazedly up and downe the streetes, calling for water, water', which didn't put the fire out. 'Shops of silkes and vellvetts' burnt, along with the stores of bread corn, 'multitudes of linnen and wollen clothes burnt to ashes; Gold and Silver melted with Brasse, Pewter and Copper'. Seventeenth-century Dorchester's reliance on agriculture, although perhaps only at peak times of the year, is demonstrated by the fire, which took place in August, and got out of control because virtually all the inhabitants were in the fields of Fordington getting in the harvest.

John White berated the consciences of the townspeople. Before the fire 'little or no money was given to any charitable use for a long season but when they saw by this sudden blast great buildings turned into heaps of stones, into dust and ashes even in a moment … many men's bowels began to yearn in compassion'. The town

established a workhouse, cannily with a brewhouse to support it, and three private almshouses were founded: Napper's Mite (1615) in South Street next to the Free School, Whetstones (1614) in Church Street, and Chubb's Almshouses (1620) in North Square. The brewhouse also provided funds for fuel for the poor in winter.

John White was not always popular in the town: in 1630 Anne Samways did speak unseemly words of Mr. White, 'Viz, that he did starve the Cuntry, and did joyne with the divell for mony, and would be a merchant and fearmer for his profitt'. There were several other prosecutions for abusing the puritan White, but generally he was respected. In 1625 Thomas Gerard considered that Dorchester 'maye justlie challenge that Superiorite of all this Shire, as well for quick Marketts and neate Buildings, as for the Number of the Inhabitants; manie of which are Men of great Wealth; and allthough it were not long

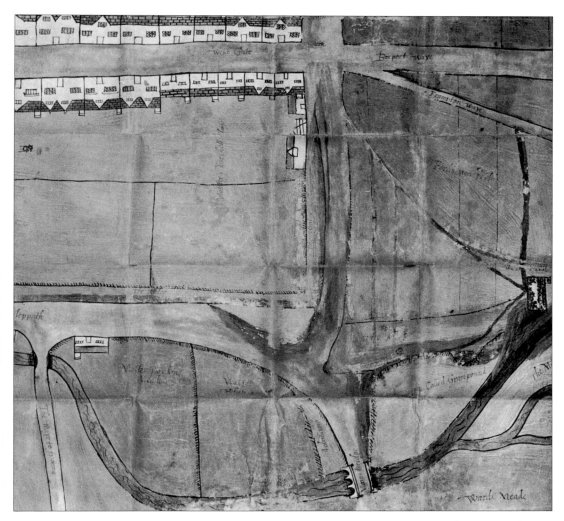

44 Part of a 17th-century map of Dorchester: the survey gives the wrong shape to the town, and the houses are probably diagrammatic, but it does given a feeling of the streets lined with houses and fields behind.

sithence much defaced with Fire, yet it is rifen up againe fairer than before'.

Dorchester had a very early library. 'A catalogue of the Bookes in the Library of Dorchester with the guivers, taken in the yeare 1631' lists a hundred books, most of them religious and puritan, but including Speed's *History of England*, and English and an Italian dictionary.

The town administration changed with new charters under James I, in 1610 and 1629. The right of the town to govern itself had gradually grown up through the centuries, being partly formalised in 1324 when Edward II gave the town a charter confirming 24 burgesses and two bailiffs. The 17th-century charters gave authority to 15 burgesses, who were actually named in the charter, and who were appointed for life. They also had the right to elect new burgesses, so those named in the charter had complete control of the present and future administration, and were a self-perpetuating oligarchy, not democratic. A mayor and six aldermen were to be elected from the council.

45 Some early 17th-century houses managed to survive all the fires of the 17th and 18th centuries. Judge Jefferies and the building next to it are timber-framed and plastered. The upper windows and the jettying out of the upper storeys are characteristic. The drawing is from 1894.

46 Dorchester also had stone houses in the 17th century: this one survived at the corner of Cornhill and Durngate Street until 1838.

The Hospital (or workhouse) was established in 1617, and all the inmates (children) made bone-lace and spun thread to off-set partly the cost of their living. The Civil War disrupted the workhouse activities and it closed for three years. It also paid for a physician for the poor. Discipline among the children there was not always very strict, with complaints in 1661 'that the pore Hospital children and others do frequently go abroad begging at dores'.

The Borough administration was much more important than the county. In the earlier 17th century, perhaps its peak time, the Borough seems to have interfered with everything which happened in the town. By the charter of 1610 it could (and did) prevent anyone who was not a freeman of the town 'to use or exercise any arte occupacion or mistery or to sell or utter any merchandize within the said Borough' except during the fairs. Even freemen of the Borough were only allowed to exercise the trade in which they were apprenticed. In 1625 Lawrence Riton, cutler, was complained of by the Saddlers 'for interloping into other mens trades, as namely, for buying and selling of raynes, bridles, and spurs, nayles, locks and other things belonging to the trade of an Ironmoner'. He was given a month to dispose of his stock.

The Borough was also quite a big landowner in the town, chiefly through its having bought chantry property when it was forcibly sold following the Reformation in the 16th century. It also administered the brewhouse and the workhouse, maintained the streets and the public wells, licensed alehouses and paid the town watchman and constables. There was no planning or limitation on building, but they were careful about encroachments onto the streets. Mr. John Browne of Frampton had to pay the town £1 for putting 'up pillars before his new house' out on the pavement in 1661. Shire Hall (despite its name) was originally used by both town and county. When it was rebuilt in 1638 the work was done by the town.

From medieval times the Borough had paid local constables to keep the town in order. They were renamed in the 17th century when the Beadle's duties were defined (1611): As to give the whippings ordered 'and to keepe all strange beggars out of the towne, and suffer no beggars to be at anie man's doores, or at the Inns, and to accuse all hedge and coppice stealers', with the

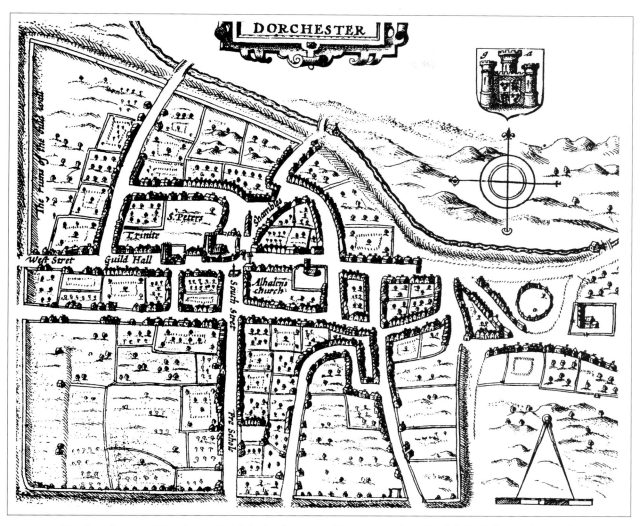

47 Speed's map of Dorchester in 1610, the first map of the town to be printed. It includes a rather crude representation of part of Fordington (right) with the pound and church prominent. The map is inaccurate, with many of the angles wrong, but shows the street pattern except for the omission of Trinity Street. The houses are a bit arbitrary: we know that High West Street was fully lined with houses, whereas this shows some gaps. The map does show the growth of the town, with back streets developing.

additional perk of keeping the stolen wood. In 1658 a Bellman was appointed 'to walke the town at night, from 12 of the clock until 5 in the morning, the sommer time; and from 12 of the clock of night until 6 in the morning the winter time'.

The Roman defences of Dorchester had been reduced to a bank all around the town, with only short stretches of the wall surviving, by the 17th century. Parts were spruced up in the Civil War, but mostly stone was robbed to re-use in new buildings. In 1668 Mr. Churchill was 'beating downe a parcell of the old towne wall' and a burgess of the town objected, 'declareing that it was pitty that part of so ancient a monument of the towne should be demolished'. The Corporation protested, but Mr. Churchill said the wall was his, and if he could not get Dorchester men to pull it down 'he would gett some out of Forthington'. It was demolished.

The 'Green walls' (as they are often called in early documents) were the territorial part of the age-long enmity between Dorchester and Fordington. In 1633 the two went to court over the division of these strips around Dorchester, with the town peevishly complaining that 'wee out of a desire for peace have long suffered the tenants [of Fordington] to incroach upon us, and they findinge our peacable dispostion have gayned more and more upon us, and by degrees have taken from us the ditches wherewith this town is surrounded and now (not therewith content) they seek to gayne from us alsoe parte of this Towne Walles'. The Borough succeeded in preserving the walls from the thieves of Fordington.

Being a Puritan area, Dorchester was on the side of Parliament in the Civil War, and was heavily fortified from the start of the war in 1642. The old Roman amphitheatre at Maumbury was adapted, and the gates had platforms for guns. The Corporation Minute Book records much detail, including the order that the town gates 'for feare of, and to prevent any danger of suprising the towne' were to be 'made fast every night at eight'. The garrison manned the gates, and kept a look-out on St Peter's tower. Refurbishing the defences cost more than £19,000, but 'one Mr Strode, a man much relied on in those parts and a man of good fortune', told the town magistrates 'that those works might keep out the Cavaliers about half an hour'. Depressed by this judgement, the town surrendered to the Royalist forces as soon as they appeared in August 1643. The surrender was particularly squalid: the garrison was already in arrears for its pay, and even before the Royalists got close the richer inhabitants of Dorchester were running away with their valuables. The garrison mutinied and then fled too.

After the restoration of the monarchy in 1660 Dorchester under Charles II gradually became less puritan. Both the ministers were removed because they would not declare their loyalty to the Church of England. The town became a livelier place and kept up with changing fashion. Maurice Gauntlett was licensed in 1679 to sell 'coffee, chacolate, sherbet or tea', only 20 years after the first coffee house opened in London.

In 1685 the Duke of Monmouth, an illegitimate son of Charles II, landed at Lyme Regis with a small force with the intention of over-throwing his Catholic uncle James II. He promised freedom to nonconformists, and they flocked to swell his army. Dorchester was only on the fringes of the Rebellion, and provided Monmouth with only a handful of recruits. Monmouth's inland march from Lyme ended with his defeat at Sedgemoor. He himself was captured in Dorset, sent to London and executed. Fifteen hundred rebels were imprisoned, and Dorchester was chosen as one of the three main centres for their trials, always known afterwards as the Bloody Assizes. Here there were 312 tried, 74 hung, and 175 transported to the Caribbean virtually as slaves. Others died waiting for trial in Dorchester. All Saints' church was used as a supplementary prison and in 1689 the parish was 'still trying to raise money towards the reparation of the church … When made a Prison for Monmouths Souldiers itt being then demolished by them'. (Parish Records).

Five

The Georgian Town

Georgian Dorchester seems to have been generally admired and seen as a desirable place to live. Daniel Defoe visited about 1716 during the travels for his *Tour Through the Whole Island of Great Britain*:

> Dorchester is indeed a pleasant agreeable town to live in, and where I thought the people seem'd less divided into factions and parties, than in other places; for though here are divisions and the people are not all of one mind, either as to religion, or politicks, yet they did not seem to separate with so much animosity as in other places: Here I saw the Church of England clergymen, and the Dissenting minister, or preacher drinking tea together, and conversing with civility and good neighbourhood: The town is populous, tho' not large, the streets broad, but the buildings old, and low; however, there is good company and a good deal of it; and a man that coveted a retreat in this world might as agreeably spend his time, and as well in Dorchester, as in any town I know in England.
>
> The downs round this town are exceeding pleasant, and come up on every side, even to the very streets end.

In the 18th century the neat and productive landscape around the town which was admired as much as the town itself. A native of Dorchester then living in London, William Gawler, had printed a long poem called simply 'Dorchester' in 1743:

> Where the expanded western Down declines,
> And silver *Frome* in fair Meanders winds,
> There stands the darling Object of my Lay,
> What lovelier View can Fancy's Self display!
> The three chief Streets one common Centre shows,
> From diff'rent Points their diff'rent Names arose,
> East, West, and South; these claim the

> Trav'ller's View,
> Neat, ancient Mansions, intermix'd with new';
> These, with the rest of more inferior Name,
> For Sweet and Cleanly yield to none in Fame.

He concludes:

> Beneath green Shades you find a cool Retreat,
> Soft Velvet Turf supports your easy Feet;
> Delightful Gardens edge the Terrace round,
> Where fragrant Flow'rs, and grateful Fruits abound;
> Thus Air, Earth, Water, ALL their Power unite
> To form a Scene of exquisite Delight,
> Which draws the Fair, the Learn'd, and the Polite;

48 Originally semi–detached, this house in Glyde Path Road is dated to 1713 by a moulded terracotta panel which also gives the owner's initials.

Here all th' adjacent Great and Gay resort,
And DORCHESTER shines, Capital and
Court.

The fair, the learned, and the polite were only a
tiny proportion of the population. They were
the ones Defoe met too, and he observed:

> The pleasant way of conversation, as it is
> manag'd among the gentlemen of this county,
> and their families, which are without
> reflection some of the most polite and well
> bred people in the isle of Britain: As their
> hospitality is very great, and their bounty to
> the poor remarkable, so their generous
> friendly way of living with, visiting, and
> associating one with another is as hard to be
> describ'd, as it is really to be admir'd; they
> seem to have a mutual confidence in, and
> friendship with one another, as if they were
> all relations.
>
> The ladies here do not want the help of
> assemblies to assist in match-making; or
> half-pay officers to run away with their
> daughters, which the meetings, call'd
> assemblies in some other parts of England,
> are recommended for. [However] the
> Dorsetshire ladies are equal in beauty, and
> may be superiour in reputation; In a word,
> their reputation seems here to be better
> kept; guarded by better conduct, and
> manag'd with more prudence, and yet the
> Dorsetshire ladies, I assure you, are not
> nuns, they do not go vail'd about streets, or
> hide themselves when visited; but a general
> freedom of conversation, agreeable, mannerly,
> kind, and good runs thro' the whole body
> of the gentry of both sexes, mix'd with the
> best of behaviour, and yet goven'd by
> prudence and modesty; such as I no where
> see better in all my observation, thro' the
> whole isle of Britain.

Defoe was writing about 1716, when assembly
rooms were very new. He would have been sorry
to know that Dorchester had them very soon
afterwards.

In the 1740s Dorchester was still admired: 'it
is a pretty large Town, and hath very wide streets;
and tho' the Buildings are neither great nor
beautiful, yet the situation is delightful, being on
a rising ground, and opening at the S. and W.
ends into sweet Fields and spacious Downs'. Later,
the author of *The Agreeable Historian, or The
Compleat Traveller* (1746) complains that 'the
houses, tho' build of Stone, are old and low' but
there are 'good Inns and a very plentiful Market

for all sorts of Provisions on Saturdays'. Hutchins
reviewed the town in the 1770s:

> One of the neatest and most agreeable in the
> county; and exceeded by few in England:
> delicately situated ... On a rising ground,
> that declines gently on the north, south and
> east. At a distance the view of the town is
> very pleasant ... The country ground around
> it is level and fruitful, abounds with arable
> and sheep pasture.
>
> A market is held here on Saturdays which
> is much lessened. Before 1730, during the
> winter, great quantities of barley were brought
> to this market. A double row of wagons
> laden with it filled the Corn Market
> [Cornhill], and a single one extended through
> the South Street, and sometimes even into
> the fields.
>
> On the breaking out of the war with
> France [1701] and the prohibition of French
> wines, brewing and malting was here carried
> to great perfection and they sent excellent
> beer to London and forign parts; but since
> 1725 thus trade is decayed. Here is now no
> staple trade of any kind carried on.

Richard Pococke, in his *Travels through England*,
described the town's economy rather more
hopefully in 1754: 'They have a manufacture of
linsey woolsey [a mixture of wool and linen or
flax] at fourteen pence a yard, they make malt,
and are famous for beer; but the chief support of
the town is the thoroughfare to Exeter, and the
nobility and gentry who live near it.'

The Borough Offender's book survives for
two years 1755-7, and this weekly court for local
complaints gives a good picture of life at the
lower end of the scale. Often the court heard no
complaints at all for four-six weeks and, if there
were cases, there was usually only one. Establish-
ing 'settlement' (that is proving that you were
born in Dorchester and could thereby claim parish
poor relief) was the commonest problem, followed by having a bastard child. Claims from
servants who had not been paid also occur: one
odd arrangement involved a man who had hired
himself as a servant at £3 or £3 10s. a year also
having 'the liberty of going out to work the
summer season' and what he earned then being
divided between himself and his master.
Occasionally the lives of individual people are
revealed as they explain why they think they
have settlement in Dorchester. Sarah Harbin was
born in the town, lived with Mrs. Gape until she

49 Georgian Dorchester was full of stables on the backlands: this one was particularly large because it served Colliton House. It was demolished in the early 1960s to make way for the library.

was ten and she went to prison for debt, and then lived with Robert Tooke, who 'took care of her Cloathed her and fed her' while 'she did his work and Errands' for three years. Aged 13, she was sent to Mrs. Edith Hellard, grocer, 'who asked her if she was willing to live with her, or words to that effect, to which [Sarah] replied that she was very glad to live with her as a servant'. Mrs. Hellard agreed to 'maintain her in Cloathes and food' and after a three weeks trial promised to give her 'wages at the rate of 30s a year'. Sarah stayed two years, but was only paid half a crown and several 'cloaths'. Ten years old was old enough to be a servant: Sarah was trying to claim settlement in Dorchester, not get her back wages.

Being a disorderly person (female); theft; tippling at time of divine service (at home); being drunk; assault; selling butter under weight; abusing and breaking windows (a woman) were all punished by fines, usually 5s. A brazier's apprentice ran away, taking one frying pan, two tea kettles and three saucepans from the brazier's stock, but he had gone too far to be punished. A woman passing through Dorchester was taken up for 'offering to tell fortunes' and put in the Blind House, the windowless lock-up by the Guildhall. William Winzar was put into the same lock-up for beating and abusing his wife, along with Edward Cox who was there 'for being drunk and abusing the Constables in the Execution of their office'. Cox was fined 5s., but Winzar was 'discharged on the request of his Wife and his promises of never offending again'. Seven women were charged with having given birth to bastard children, and one man was prosecuted for playing cards.

The settlement papers for All Saints parish survive, and show us how people moved around the county. Occasionally people had gone further:

50 South Street about 1860, still with Georgian houses (not shops). Most of these brick fronts were applied to older houses in the late 18th century to bring them up to date. South Street was purely residential until the railways arrived: the High Street was the main through road with shops.

Jane Gaylard, who had lived in Dorchester with her parents until she was 35, moved to London about 1715. There she had worked in shoe making, as a laundress, as a 'seller of oysters about the streets' and finally as 'a cleaner of Gentlemen's rooms in Grays Inn'. She married an Irishman, who died while both were working as servants, and when she became ill and chargeable to the parish in 1730 they sent her back to Dorchester. Her story is preserved only because she failed, but it demonstrates the way people moved around.

Dorchester had been an important stop on the road to the west from Roman times, and this continued in the medieval period. These routes were greatly improved from the 1750s with the turnpike system. Instead of the parishes maintaining the roads, turnpike trust companies were formed. They charged tolls on road-users and used the money to maintain and improve the routes. The Harnham, Blandford and Dorchester Trust improved the roads to Blandford and to Bridport from 1764, making radical alterations in the 1820s including lowering Yellowham Hill

51 & 52   Grey's Bridge, built in 1748 (and seen above about 1910, with men cutting the river weed to improve the fishing; Dorchester is to the right), made the biggest change to the road pattern before the bypass. Before it was constructed all the traffic went through Fordington as the map shows. The new road is shown on the map. Grey's Bridge is on the first river; the second river is much smaller than the map implies. This map of 1746 from the Fordington Court Rolls shows the old road through Fordington and the projected line of the new road.

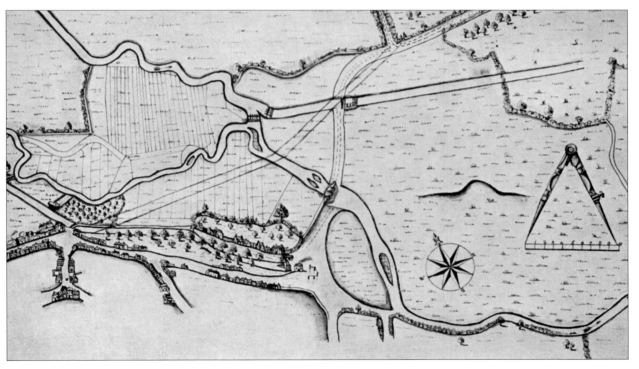

53 Cottages dating from the second half of the 18th century at the top of The Grove were demolished in 1959. Georgian buildings were not all sophisticated brick town houses: these stone cottages were originally five small separate dwellings. Photograph about 1909.

just to the east of Dorchester. The Weymouth, Melcombe Regis and Dorchester Trust ran the roads to Weymouth and to the north of Dorchester from 1761, and in 1768 the Dorchester & Wool Trust turnpiked the road to Wareham. These trusts ran their roads until the mid-19th century, by which time the railways had taken over most long-distance traffic.

The old workhouse stopped functioning in the late 17th century, and in 1744 a meeting of the three parishes of Dorchester decided that a new workhouse was needed so that the 'Poor may be maintained therein at less expense than they are at present ... and the Aged and inform

Poor will be more comfortably and suitably provided for'. Those 'who are of ability to labour may under proper regulation be usefully and beneficially employed, and the children who now do little but beg like Vagabonds from door to door will not only be instructed in honest Industry and labour, but likewise be Bred up in Sentiments of Religion and Virtue'. There were thereby hopes for a 'Reformation' in the town, abolishing the 'Debauched and ruinous Habit of Drinking Gin and other Spiritous Liquors, a habit which hath not only corrupted the morals, but also ruined the constitutions of many of our Poor'.

54 Inside West Mill, West Fordington, with two stones being fed with grain to be ground, and sacks of grain left. This mill was grinding flour throughout Georgian times.

The workhouse was at the south end of South Street, and is shown on Hutchins' map. Although there were periodic complaints about the cost (31 inmates in 1750; cost for the year £122), it continued functioning until 1837, when the Poor Law Union Workhouse (catering for a much wider area than just Dorchester) was built. The contents of the town workhouse (including '4 broad Bottom chairs' and 31 beds) was sold at auction, and the land was redeveloped as housing.

By the late 18th century Dorchester had assemblies, and even theatres. Travelling companies had visited the town since the 16th century (although in 17th-century Puritan Dorchester they were not always welcome) and used Shire Hall, but from the 1780s other buildings were converted, including a riding school. Religion, too was becoming more diverse.

There had been Baptists and Quakers in the town from the 17th century, but in the 18th century there were several more nonconformist sects. Hutchins' map of 1774 shows a Dissenters' Meeting House in Colliton Street, and another opened in Durngate Street in 1776.

In the 1790s the town must have been full of builders and labourers because there were so many public buildings being constructed. Both the Town Hall and Shire Hall were rebuilt, and a large new prison and barracks constructed. Dorchester had had a prison since medieval times, first in the middle portion of High East Street, and at the lower end of the street from 1633. This had been rebuilt in 1784, but with new ideas about prison hygiene and administration emerging at this time it was out-dated before it was finished. The prison reformer Howard persuaded the county to rebuild on a much larger

55 The view from Poundbury in 1796, with West Mill (see p.45) centre and the town in the distance right showing the abrupt edge between town and country, marked by the trees of the Walks. The water meadows clearly show the patterns of runnels used to cover them with water in the late winter.

56 Dorchester from the east in the 1770s, from Hutchins' *History of Dorset*. The new road leads out over the watermeadows extreme left, and the pattern of houses along the streets and gardens behind is clear. The three churches are shown, but one is oddly placed. Well-dressed citizens adorn the meadows.

57 Shire Hall, built in 1797 for the then tiny county administration. It was also used as a court, and even for balls and public entertainments. There was much building in Dorchester in the late 18th century: besides Shire Hall, the Prison, the Barracks and the Town Hall were all rebuilt in the 1790s, along with the re-fronting of many private houses.

scale on a new site, an empty field once occupied by the castle. It was completed in 1795, and was a model prison for its date, costing more than £16,000. The buildings inside the wall were rebuilt in 1884. The prison held all the offenders of the county, and public executions there were popular entertainment.

Many of the houses in the middle of Dorchester are Georgian survivors, built by the gentry and tradespeople of the town. Although visitors such as Fanny Burney, who was 'diverted much by its comic, irregular old houses' in 1791, wrote of its old-fashioned aspects, local writers

extolled the improvements and modern buildings of the town. Hutchins in 1774 wrote, 'The buildings are chiefly of brick and stone, except some Flemish building of plaister and timber in the Corn Market and about St Peter's.' Visitors must have preferred describing this picturesque part, locals the more modern remainder. The Cupola, an octagonal building on pillars whose open lower storey sheltered part of the market, was built in the middle of Cornhill some time before 1714 when the town paid for it to be illuminated with candles. Sadly, it became dilapidated and was demolished in 1783. The

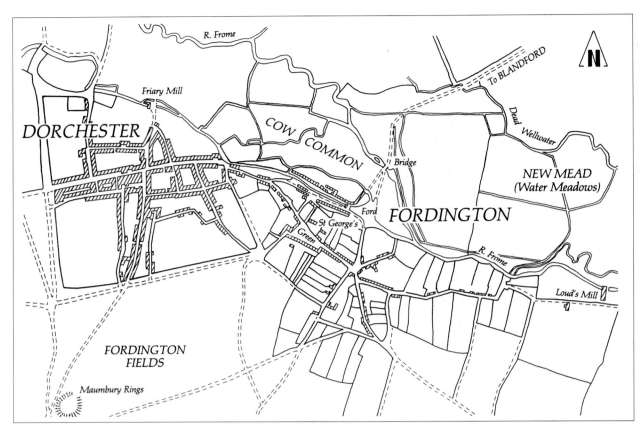

58 Dorchester and Fordington, showing the road system as it was before Grey's Bridge was built in 1748 along with a new road directly from the end of High East Street. The old route was through Fordington, along by the river, through the ford at the mill, and across a bridge a little downstream from Grey's Bridge. The new road completely by-passed Fordington. The small enclosures around the village (clearly shown as hedged on the original map) contrast with the edge of Fordington Field, where even the tracks are unfenced. (Based on Simpson's map of 1779.)

Borough and county then each constructed new buildings in the 1790s, the county rebuilding Shire Hall in its present form but allowing the town to use the hall for meetings, 'balls or any other public entertainment'. Troops quartered in the town were allowed the hall as a guard room. The Borough built an impressive Classical town hall on a new site next to St Peter's church. Sometimes older buildings were demolished to make way for the new, but fires continued to trouble the town. In 1725, 57 houses in South Street, Trinity Street and Charles Street were destroyed and, in 1775, another 40, 'chiefly the habitations of poor people' in High East Street and area. The fire 'raged with great fury for several hours, making great havoc amongst the thatched houses,

and passing those which were roofed with tiles or slates'.

Little or no work was done on the churches during the 18th century, but the churchwarden's accounts for All Saints show an increasing respect for the dignity of the church. In 1700 it was agreed not to let the churchyard any more, 'it being found by Experiance that the Letting theoff & Suffring persons to Dry Cloath there have bin to the Damage off the Parishoners by breaking up of Church Windows and other abuses'.

By the 18th century the walls were no longer needed as defences, and were laid out as elegant tree-lined walks, with the top flattened out. They were then on the edge of the town,

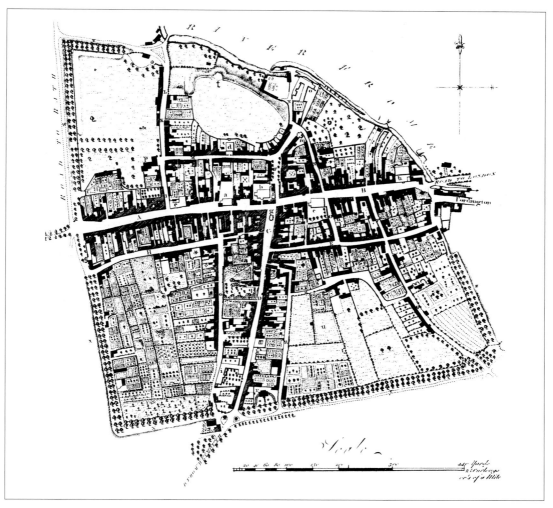

59 Dorchester from Hutchins' *History of Dorset*. This map cost the Borough £15-19s. in 1772 and,
strictly, covers only the area of the town. It is remarkably accurate. The main buildings are lettered: (a),
(b) and (c) are the churches, with St Peter's having buildings between it and the road. These were
demolished around 1800. In Colliton Street (then Pease Lane) is the Dissenter's Meeting House (d), built
in 1718 by the Unitarians (now demolished and replaced by Jubilee Court). Shire Hall is (e) on High
West Street. The little building to the right of St Peter's Church (f) is the Guildhall of the Borough,
replaced twenty years later by a much larger one. The Cupola (g) in the middle of Cornhill was a market
house. The County Jail (h) was still at the end of High Street. The buildings across the street were
demolished later in the 18th century. At the bottom of South Street, running through to Trinity Street
(then called South Back Street and not continuing through as a road to High East Street) was the
Borough Workhouse (i). Just up South Street is the Free or Grammar School (k). The three almshouses
of the town are (l), (m) and (n). Napper's Mite in South Street (next to the Grammar School) and
Chubbs Almshouses (m), North Square and Whetstones (n) in Church Street. In the north of the town
(t) marks the site of the Castle, still empty, and to the right (o) is the Friary, converted to a house. The
buildings between them are Friary Mill. To the left is Colliton House (p) with its huge grounds. Other
houses are identified: halfway down South Street, on the left is a house with large grounds marked (q)
which was Cedar Court, and South Lodge to the right of the end of South Street is (r). The open field
in East and West Walls have become gardens or little paddocks by the time of this map, and one in the
east marked (u) is the bowling green. All the walks are in place, although Colliton Walk is obviously
recent as it is called New Walk.

60   The Barracks, now called the Artillery Barracks, built in 1795 at a cost of £24,000. These buildings were damaged by fire in the 1920s and only one block survives, much altered.

61   Looking along South Walks, 1950s. The chestnut trees make this part of the walks particularly pretty.

62 The riverside path along the Frome, also good for trees, in the 1950s.

with only a couple of houses outside them. They were planted in two separate campaigns: the west (West Walks and Colliton Walk) and part of the south (Bowling Alley Walk) about 1712, and South Walk with Salisbury Fields in 1743. Some of the land and the planting was paid for by local inhabitants, all the walks being open for the public. Fordington manor had to be placated too; they moaned about losing four acres in 1712 and tried to prosecute the Borough. And in 1743, a Fordington tenant had to be bribed out of some of the land. The original trees were sycamores and limes in the earlier plantings, and horse chestnuts in the later. The riverside walk completes the circuit of the town, which became the citizens' favourite promenade.

Dorchester's avenues of trees on all the approach roads were as famous as the walks, but most of them have gone either because of development or elm disease. They were planted from the 1770s, and at their peak ran right up the Bridport Road to the position of the by-pass, along Weymouth Road to well beyond the current bypass, and along the London Road. The only one currently impressive avenue is along Wareham Road, where the original planting of 1888 was alternate red and white chestnuts. Even this is a bit patchy and does not fit the current road pattern. Part of the London road across the water meadows is good. In the early 20th century there was a Dorchester Avenues Society specifically to protect and nurture them.

Six

The Town 1800-1850

The first half of the 19th century is one of the most interesting periods in Dorchester's history. The town started to become industrialised and huge numbers of buildings were constructed. It was a nodal point for coaches, and at the peak of the system in 1839 coaches called at the town 96 times a week or 16 a day, as none ran on Sundays. Four coaches ran to London daily, the fastest, the Royal Mail, taking 13½ hours. They took different routes via Salisbury, Southampton, Wimborne or Poole, and one continued to Exeter. There were daily services to and from Bath, Bristol and Weymouth, and every other day to Taunton and Exeter.

The most important coach was the mail coach, which carried the post. The system was established in 1784, and Dorchester was on one of the two routes to the west. They kept up a steady seven-eight miles per hour, which was then regarded as miraculous. The slowest long-distance transport was the wagons which carried goods and passengers who could only afford the cheapest fares. They moved only a couple of miles an hour, less than walking pace. In 1827 five different firms were running wagons through Dorchester, with at least two a day leaving for London, Exeter, Bath (or Bristol) and more to Weymouth. The railways changed the pattern

63 From a bill of 1844. The *Mail Coach Inn* was in North Square and had nothing at all to do with the mail coach, which used the *King's Arms*. The only carrier to use the *Mail Coach* was one from Cerne Abbas: they called themselves the *Mail Coach* because it was glamorous and up-to-date. The coach in the engraving is a proper mail coach.

64 Three views of train travel near Dorchester in 1872, from *Our Journal At Winterborne St Martins*: comfortable travelling; over-crowded travelling; and being made to enter an already full carriage, to laughter from the occupants.

of the coaches even before they reached Dorchester. In 1840 the Railway Coach was the easiest way to reach London—leaving Dorchester at 6a.m. it met the 1 o'clock train at Southampton so that the passenger reached London at 5p.m.

A railway from Dorchester to Weymouth was proposed in 1834, only four years after the first railway in the world opened between Liverpool and Manchester, but this came to nothing. The line from London to Southampton opened in 1840, and in 1847 it was extended to

Dorchester. The Weymouth line opened in 1857. The first timetable shows five trains a day to Southampton, but only four of them linked through to London. The best time to London was 6½ hours.

In many places the arrival of the railway heralded huge growth, but this was not the case in Dorchester. The town had always been a nodal point in the era of coaches, and the population increased very little from 1841 to 1871. This was partly because there was little or no land available for building, but the failure

65 Loud's Mill had been a cloth mill, originally for fulling or thickening woollen cloth, from the time it was first built in the 1590s. It was rebuilt on this huge scale in 1825 by William Stanton, and was demolished in the 1980s.

of the textile industries didn't help. Loud's Mill at Fordington was rebuilt on a large scale in 1825 as a cloth factory, producing woollen cloth. It continued working until the middle of the 19th century, but the trade had moved to the north of England and the mill was not a great success.

A four-storey soda-water manufactory was built in Trinity Street in the 1830s, and a reporter in the *Chronicle* in July 1835 refers to the 'spirit manifested in this town of late' for improvement. He particularly admired Davis & Sons Soda Water Manufactory, where 'they have lately erected a steam engine of considerable power, by which the whole of their apparatus is set in motion. [This] and the new and extensive building, are amongst the most complete works of the kind in the Kingdom.' It really looked as though

Dorchester was going to become a manufacturing area.

Up to the middle of the 19th century brewing in Dorchester was only on a small scale, and the town with its traditional cloth industry was basically still the trading centre for a rural area. A small theatre was built in North Square in 1807, and became an Assembly Rooms but didn't last very long as the competition from card assemblies at the *Antelope* was too great. The building was used as a store and demolished in the 1980s. The best equipped theatre was the Loyalty, built in 1828 behind the *Antelope*, running along the Trinity Street frontage towards High West Street. It had a proper stage, traps for footlights and a gallery. After it closed in 1843 it too was used as a store, and was demolished in 1965.

66 New types of buildings appeared in towns in the early 19th century, including banks who wanted solid buildings to impress their customers. The pedimented building left was built for the Old Dorchester Bank in 1835, and the building on the right was used by Bower and Eliot, another bank. The photograph shows High West Street in 1874: all the buildings in the centre were about to be demolished.

Dorchester had had its own workhouse from 1774, but in 1837 the Union Workhouse was built just outside the town to the west, the one in *Far from the Madding Crowd*, a place dreaded by the poor. The 1837 workhouses were deliberately harsh places, designed to deter the poor. They were supposed to offer a worse life than outside, but this was difficult in Dorset in the 1830s, when labourers' wages meant virtual starvation. By the 1920s children were no longer housed there, but it continued in use for the elderly and for tramps, being taken over by the County Council in 1930. In 1948 it became Damer's Hospital, and is now offices and a children's nursery.

The new workhouse may actually have been better than the old one. Someone wrote to the *Dorset County Chronicle* in October 1846 about having seen the children from Dorchester Workhouse, 'all neatly dressed and remarkably clean', out on Fordington Down 'with cheerful faces'. The master had taken them there 'to enjoy the fresh and salubrious air of the downs and to gambol'. The writer contrasted this modern treatment with 'the old parish house, where they were brought up in habits of idleness and filth, without control … In ignorance and disorderly manners'. He then continues, 'The young females are likely to make good and useful servants, cleanly in their habits and instructed in the common duties of life'.

Contemporaries recognised many changes in the town in the first half of the 19th century. Lucia Boswell Stone remembered the street

67 The Dorford Baptist Chapel, a plain building of 1830 with a surprising curved front whose line is continued by the yard to the right and the house beyond which also dates from around 1830. It was called the Dorford chapel because it was at the junction of *Dor*chester and *Ford*ington.

lighting in the early 19th century, before the gas came: people carried lanterns because 'the oil lamps were very dim, and were often blown out by the frequent high winds'. She herself was collected if she was out after dark by a servant with a large glass lantern who walked in front of her 'casting light upon the puddles, with which our ill-paved streets were full after a shower'.

Lucia Boswell Stone was born in High West Street in 1806. As a young person she found the town dull with an 'old-world quiet aspect', the only excitements being the fairs and the assize courts. The latter were attended by the gentry as

an entertainment. In the 1810s there were supposed to be more old maids in Dorchester than any other town in the county. In the 1820s High West Street was completely residential, with no shops. Several families who lived there had carriages and powdered footmen. A watchman walked the town all night, calling the hour: 'Past ten o'clock, and a rainy night'. She remembered going as a child to services in St Peter's church before it was restored, sitting in a huge oak pew and peering out through the railings. The singing gallery was used by the choir and their band of three violins and a cello, and they led all the singing.

She thought their social gatherings and simple amusements presented a 'vivid contrast' to those of later Victorian times. 'There were no set dinners … the townsfolk were very friendly and hospitable, but the times would not permit extravagance, and dinner with the corner dishes and profusion of modern days would have been thought the height of folly then.' Most entertaining consisted of tea-parties, starting at 6p.m. with tea and coffee, followed by games or cards punctuated with offerings of wine, cake and biscuits. These decorous parties finished at 10p.m. The only exceptions were the annual county balls which were 'strictly aristocratic', although some townspeople crept in. Formal quadrilles were danced, and sometimes a country dance 'in a sober stately measure', but never the wicked new waltz.

68 Many boundary stones were erected in 1835 to mark the new, extended borough, with Municipal Bounds of the Borough of Dorchester on their cast-iron plates. In 1901 the *Chronicle* described them as 'none too ornamental' and looking like milestones.

69 Looking down High West Street in about 1860, with the short-lived Holy Trinity Church, built in 1824 in light-hearted Regency Gothic style, having odd corner turrets like chimneys. It was demolished in 1875.

70 The Town Hall (centre) was again rebuilt in 1848, this time leaving a space for the road between itself and St Peter's Church. Like the old one, the new building was open underneath to accommodate market stalls.

As a county town, Dorchester has always been a centre for courts, and it was on account of its judicial function that it became famous (or infamous) in 1834. The Tolpuddle Martyrs were known at the time as the Dorchester Unionists, or by their supporters as the Dorchester Labourers. They were arrested in 1834 not for forming a union (that was legal), but for administering an illegal oath, although this was just a legal fiction for attacking Trades Unions. The Tolpuddle men were not even trying to get their meagre wages raised; they were trying to prevent them being lowered again. Before 1832 they had been earning 9s. (45p) a week as

agricultural labourers, but the wage had been lowered to 6s. (30p) in 1833. The farmers blamed the agricultural depression, but it was not possible for families to live on the wages. The six Tolpuddle men were arrested, put in the County Prison at Dorchester and then tried at the Crown Court. Their leader's statement from the dock was doubtless influenced by his having been a Methodist lay preacher: 'We have injured no man's reputation, character, person or property. We were uniting together to protect ourselves, our wives, and our children, from utter degradation and starvation.' They were transported to Australia, but enormous outcry at

71   The Dorset County Hospital about 1860. This was started in 1840, and looks like a large manor house. It has only recently ceased to act as the town hospital.

their unfair trial led to their being pardoned, and they returned to England. The outcry was from London and the north, not from Dorset, and even the financial support for the wives and children was not raised locally.

Fordington grew enormously in the first half of the 19th century, from 888 people in 1801 to 2,937 in 1841. Labourers were leaving the land because of the agricultural depression, and moving to the towns. A small area of Fordington down by the river was freehold, and this was divided and sub-divided until it was covered with cottages, many of them inhabited by several families. The General Board of Health in 1830 re-

ported favourably on Dorchester, which had 'an almost total want of the poorer sort of houses, the lower class of inhabitants being confined chiefly to Fordington'. By 1854 the population density of this little area was higher than that of Manchester: more than 1,000 people in two or three small streets. The Mill Street area was described by Hardy in *The Mayor of Casterbridge* as 'the hiding place of those who are in distress, in debt, and trouble of every kind ... Much that was sad, much that was low, some things that were baneful, could be seen in Mixen Lane. Vice ran freely in and out of certain of the doors of the neighbourhood.'

72 Some of the few working-class houses built in Dorchester in the 1830s in the lower part of The Grove (since demolished). They are architecturally very simple and plain, but they were later held up as bad examples of development because they had no water supply or drainage.

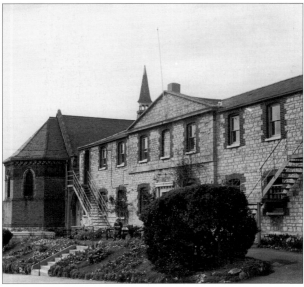

73 The Union Workhouse was built on the outskirts of the town in 1836. This is only the front block: behind was a large building on the plan of a Greek cross. This photograph is from the 1960s.

74 Small courts and terraces filled the area behind Mill Street, Fordington in the early 19th century. These were photographed shortly before they were demolished in the 1930s.

75 The farmyard behind the church at Fordington in the 1850s. All the farmyards were actually in the village because the land was still farmed on the open-field system. 'Here wheat-ricks overhung the old Roman street, and thrust their eaves against the church tower; green-thatched barns, with doorways as high as the gates of Solomon's temple, opened directly upon the main thoroughfare. Barns indeed were so numerous as to alternate with every half-dozen houses along the way.' (From *The Mayor of Casterbridge*.)

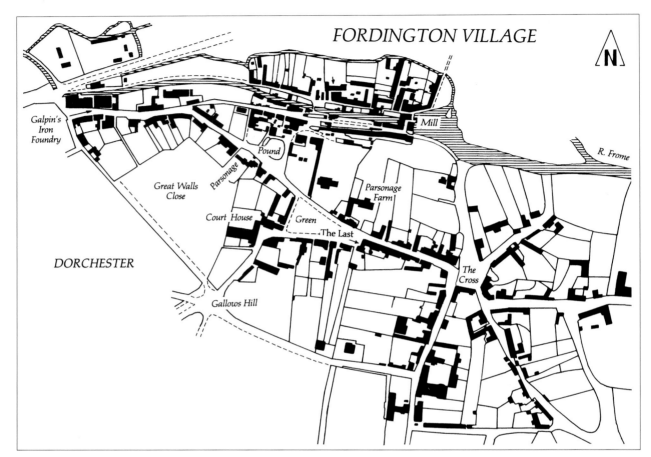

76 Fordington from the Tithe map of 1841. The pattern of farms and small closes in the village (right) is very clear, with the church, court house, pound and pub (the *Last*, presumably the cobbler's last) all close to the Green. The Mill Street area is already densely occupied. Galpin's Iron Foundry at the bottom of the High Street later became Lott & Walne.

In 1849 and 1854 cholera broke out in Fordington, and only the heroic efforts of Henry Moule, vicar of Fordington, prevented it spreading to Dorchester. He wrote public letters to Prince Albert, then administering the Duchy, to try to get the housing in Fordington improved. Unaccountably, in view of his zeal for reform elsewhere, Prince Albert did nothing. Fordington remained an agricultural village with an urban slum attached until the open fields were enclosed in 1874.

Seven

Casterbridge – Hardy's Town

Suddenly in the middle of the 19th century Dorchester comes alive: Thomas Hardy's novels *The Mayor of Casterbridge* and *Far from the Madding Crowd* fill the town with what seem to be real people, and from 1860 there are photographs which show what it was really like.

Hardy was born at Bockhampton, only two miles down the river Frome from Dorchester. In 1850, when he was ten years old, he attended a nonconformist school in Greyhound Yard, off South Street, walking in every day. He knew every corner of the town, and when he was

77 High West Street about 1860. The pillared porch is part of the *King's Arms* where the public dinner in *The Mayor of Casterbridge* was held. Hardy made notes on local matters and one lists the sites of Dorchester post office: in the 1830s it was inside 'the door above the King's Arms arch. In my childhood it was at the door below the King's Arms', but by the time this photograph was taken it had moved to South Street. Hardy took pleasure in chronicling alterations in the town.

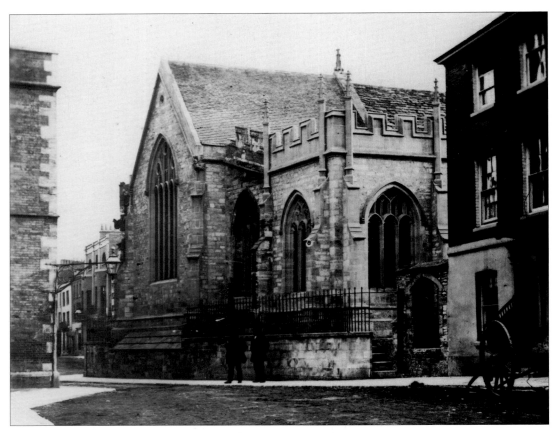

78 North Square in about 1860, looking at St Peter's Church. Butchers had their stalls here from medieval times, but by 1860 they had mostly moved into shops in the area. Hardy worked on the restoration of St Peter's Church in 1856.

given the Freedom of the Borough of Dorchester in 1910, he said in his speech of acceptance 'that the freedom of the Borough of Dorchester did seem to me at first something that I had possessed a long while - had helped myself to, to speak plainly'. Schoolchildren know their town better than anyone, especially, if, like Hardy, their school is central.

Hardy worked in Dorchester as an apprentice architect for five years from the age of 16, so for those most impressionable years from 10 to 21 he was at school or working in the town. *The Mayor of Casterbridge*, Hardy's tenth novel, was published in 1886 but is set in the 1850s or '60s, the time he knew the town as a child and young man. His descriptions show a huge knowledge and understanding of how the town worked, as well as a native's infatuation with the place:

Casterbridge, as has been hinted, was a place deposited in the block upon a corn-field. There was no suburb in the modern sense, or transitional inter-mixture of town and down. It stood, with regard to the wide fertile land adjoining, clean-cut and distinct, like a chess-board on a green table-cloth. The farmer's boy could sit under his barley-mow and pitch a stone into the office-window of the town-clerk; reapers at work among the sheaves nodded to acquaintances standing on the pavement-corner; the red-robed judge, when he condemned a sheep-stealer, pronounced sentence to the tune of Baa, that floated in at the window from the remainder of the flock browsing hard by; and at executions the waiting crowd stood in a meadow immediately before the drop, out of which the cows had been temporarily driven to give the spectators room.

79 The chestnut trees of South Walks about 1860. The very tall man wears a stove-pipe hat and is clearly a gentleman. The Walks were kept for pedestrians even then, with iron railings to keep vehicles out.

He understood the rural basis of its economy in 1860:

> Casterbridge was in most respects but the pole, focus, or nerve-knot of the surrounding country life; differing from the many manufacturing towns which are as foreign bodies set down, like boulders on a plain in a green world with which they have nothing in common. Casterbridge lived by agriculture at one remove further from the fountain-head than the adjoining villages—no more. The townsfolk understood every fluctuation in the rustic's condition, for it affected their receipts as much as the labourer's; they entered into the troubles and joys which moved the aristocratic families ten miles round—for the same reason. And even at the dinner-parties for the professional families the subjects of discussion were corn, cattle-disease, sowing and reaping, fencing and planting; while politics were viewed by them less from their own standpoint of burgesses with rights and privileges than from the standpoint of their county neighbours.

Dorchester in 1860 had 6,823 inhabitants, half in the town, half in Fordington. Many more people visited the town for fairs and markets. In 1890 Hardy complained of the little known about the town of Roman Dorchester:

> Where stood the large buildings, how did the roofs group themselves, what were the gardens like, if any, what social character had the streets, what were the customary noises … Were the passengers up and down the ways few in number, or did they ever form a busy throng such as we now see on a market day?

For mid-19th-century Dorchester Hardy supplies many of the answers to these questions: behind the drama of the principal characters is seen the life of the town. When the 8 o'clock curfew bell was rung in the evening, for example, 'it was utilised by the inhabitants as a signal for shutting their shops … a clatter of shutters arose through the whole length of the High Street'. Soon afterwards the shopkeepers and their assistants came 'out for a whiff of air' joining the other lower-class street idlers. All were looking to see what was going on, if anything.

The Saturday market was held in the centre of the town, with farmers selling corn from samples.

80 The south end of South Street about 1860, just becoming the main entrance to the town after both the railway stations were built on this side. South Street was still mainly residential, but the increase in traffic caused by the stations helped it to become a shopping street. Lewer's Carriage Works was an early industrial building with huge windows.

'Here they surged on this one day of the week, forming a little world of leggings, switches, and sample-bags.' But the other streets were full too:

> Horses for sale were tied in rows, their forelegs on the pavement, their hind legs in the street, in which position they occasionally nipped little boys by the shoulder who were passing to school. And any inviting recess in front of a house that had been modestly kept back from the general line was utilized by pig-dealers as a pen for their stock.

Had Hardy been nipped on the shoulder on his way to school? Even on non-market days the streets were full of interest:

> The old-fashioned fronts of these houses, which had older than old-fashioned backs, rose sheer from the pavement, into which the bow-windows protruded like bastions … [Other obstructions included] door-steps, scrapers, cellar-hatches, church buttresses, and the overhanging angles of walls which, originally unobtrusive, had become bow-legged and knock-kneed.

Carriers vans from all the villages around 'were drawn up on each side of the street in close file, so as to form at places a wall between pavement and the roadway'. The life of the *Three Mariners Inn*, High East Street, is described in great detail by Hardy:

81 The Old Grammar School (right) and Napper's Mite almshouses, South Street in about 1860. Hardy was working as an architect in one of the Georgian houses just visible on the left when the photograph was taken. South Street at this time was still almost entirely residential. One-fifth of the 105 professional and other upper- and middle-class families listed as 'private residents' in the 1860 *Directory* lived in South Street.

A long, narrow, dimly-lit passage gave access to the inn, within which passage the horses going to their stalls at the back, and the coming and departing human guests, rubbed shoulders indiscriminately, the latter running no slight risk of having their toes trodden upon by the animals. The good stabling and the good ale of the Mariners, though somewhat difficult to reach on account of there being but this narrow way to both, were nevertheless perseveringly sought out by the sagacious old heads who knew what was what in Casterbridge.

In some of this Hardy seems to be reflecting a slightly earlier town. He refers to 'the two feeble old' constables, but by the 1850s Dorchester

had Borough Police. His descriptions of life in the fictional *Three Mariners* reflects reports of the town in the 1820s. At Christmas 1829,

a party of soldiers were drinking in the Three Mariners public-house in company with a number of men, inhabitants of the town and Fordington; when, a dispute having arisen on some trivial subject, words soon gave way to blows, and the soldiers drawing their swords, attacked the townsmen without distinction and wounded several very seriously. The others procured spits, pokers, pitchforks or any weapon they could lay their hands on and a general melée ensued.

The soldiers retreated back up the High Street

82 & **83**   The two sides of Cornhill about 1860. While the rest of South Street was residential, Cornhill was full of shops and had one of the main coaching inns, the *Antelope*, centre in the lower photograph.

84 The *Three Mariners*, East Street, drawn by Thomas Hardy. The old building was demolished later in the 19th century. 'The bay window projecting into the street, whose interior was so popular among the frequenters of the inn, was closed with shutters, in each of which appeared a heart-shaped aperture. 'A four-centred Tudor arch was over the entrance, and over the arch the signboard. Being on the sunny side of the street, the three comrades had suffered largely from warping, splitting, fading, and shrinkage, so that they were but a half-invisible film upon the reality of the grain, and knots, and nails which composed the signboard.' (From *The Mayor of Casterbridge*.)

85 Looking up Bridport Road from Top o'Town about 1860, before any houses were built. Top o'Town House is right, and the Bridport Road Avenue directly ahead, with the open fields of Fordington left.

'cutting at everyone in their progress and pelted by the populace with stones etc.'. Amazingly no-one was killed.

An incident probably involving Hardy's uncle, who lived in Fordington, seems even more like an episode from a novel. On Christmas Eve 1827 John Hardy, who belonged to the 'Bockington' band, 'was in the kitchen of the Phoenix Inn, with the remainder of the band. Whilst there a set of mummers, from Fordington, came to the door, and one of them knocked

the drum-stick' out of Hardy's hand. He was then struck with a wooden sword (one of the mummers' props) and knocked down several times in the street, leaving him 'much Bruised'. Doubtless, competition for patonage between the mummers and the band (not a church band as it had drums, and not the one Hardy's grandfather, John's father, organised at Stinsford) was at the bottom of this incident.

Perambulators were invented in the 1870s, and by 1876 a letter to the local paper

86   Two prams with attendant nursemaids in High West Street, 1891. The coachman and trap are probably waiting for someone shopping in Genges to the right.

87 From earliest times up to the 1950s animals being driven through the town were a hazard, and occasionally got into places they weren't wanted. Here a heifer emerges from Dyers grocers in High East Street in 1954. Three had wandered into the shop and exited through the passage to the house front door.

complained of the 'abominable nuisance, the wheeling of perambulators on the pavement … the chances are ten to one that you [the pedestrian] get your shins barked'. The complainer had seen 'a modern chariot race, between four of these ladies, down a narrow back street' in Dorchester, and the young nurse maids continued along the pavement, driving him into the gutter 'while they had what appeared a most enlivening, if not improving, gossip'. Those who were rich enough to buy perambulators were also rich enough to employ people to look after their children.

The Candlemas (14 February) hiring fair was described by Hardy in *Far from the Madding Crowd* (1874): 'At one end of the street stood from three to four hundred blithe and hearty labourers waiting upon Chance.' The hiring fair was the main method of getting a new job for the labourers. Hardy paints a happy picture of

the fair, but in 1868, a little later than the period in which the novel is set, the *Dorset County Chronicle* stated that the hiring fair had 'been justly deprecated as a nuisance'. 'As usual a motley mob of labourers of all descriptions congregated in High West Street for hire; and, although the baneful system has been spoken against and depreciated in every possible way by farmers, the supply of labour did not seem to be in the least degree abated, compared with former years.' Many failed to get new jobs, and 'later in the day there were the usual scenes of intemperance and excess which render this fair so objectionable'. The newspaper seems mostly to be objecting to large numbers of labourers ('such a set of roughs') coming to the town, and the pick-pockets who followed the crowds of farmers and labourers.

Hardy compared the Candlemas hiring fair of the 1850s with that of the 1880s,

88   One of the earliest photographs of Dorchester, dated 1856. The North Square entranceway to the
Prison, demolished later in the 19th century. Hardy saw Martha Browne hung in public here in 1856. He
stood close to the gallows which were set up on the top of this gate, in a huge crowd of people.

spot-lighting the changes in clothing: in the 1850s one saw

a crowd whose general colour was whity-brown flecked with white. Black was almost absent, the few farmers who wore that shade being hardly discernible. Now the crowd is as dark as a London crowd. This change is owing to the rage for cloth clothes which possesses the labourers of to-day. Formerly they came in smock-frocks and gaiters, the shepherds with their crooks, the carters with a zone of whipcord round their hats, thatchers with a straw tucked into the brim, and so on. Now, with the exception of the crook in the hands of an occasional old shepherd, there is no mark of speciality in the groups, who might be tailors or under-takers, men for what they exhibit externally. Out of a group of eight, for example, who talk together in the middle of the road, only one wears corduroy trousers. Two wear cloth pilot-coats and black trousers, two patterned tweed suits with black canvas overalls, the remaining four suits being of faded broadcloth.

The Dorsetshire Labourer (1883)

Eight

Late Victorian and Edwardian Dorchester

The greatest physical change to Dorchester in the second half of the century was the enclosure in 1874 of the open fields of Fordington, which finally allowed the town to expand outside the Roman defences. Fordington became part of the Duchy of Cornwall in the 17th century, and most of the land is still owned by the Prince of Wales. The Duchy proposed enclosing Fordington in 1801, but the tenants rejected this. The old open field system did not fit with 19th-century ideas of efficiency. Mr. T. Fisher, a Fordington farmer, urged enclosure in 1813, complaining that the system hadn't changed for 'hundreds of years' and that the 'prodigious waste of time of harvest, by trampling over standing corn, to come at different pieces is beyond calculation'. He thought yields could be increased, but also felt the old system had 'no trifling influence on the morals of the lower class of the people who can commit petty thefts with less chance of detection'. Enclosure would also prevent the uppity small-holders roaming 'over 3,000 acres of ground with 4 horses committing trespass and depredations'. Clearly such an easy-going system could not last, and in 1842 the Duchy announced that it would

not allow any more lifeholds. The lands had been copyhold tenure, that is a lease was given for three lives but the people had to be named at the time of the lease, and fines were charged for adding new lives. It took until 1874 for all the leases to fall in, and then the Duchy divided the land into five farms.

The enclosure completely changed Fordington and it gave Dorchester the opportunity at last to burst out of the corset of the Roman defences. Large houses were built in Prince of Wales Road and Great Western Road, and terraces in Fordington (Duke's Avenue) and the Cornwall Road area. From 1896 the much larger area of Victoria Park was started to the south-west of the town, with terraced houses in the northern part and large detached houses in Queen's Avenue. By 1906 Frederick Treves was complaining that 'all around the grey old town [of Dorchester] are arising those florid suburbs which in days to come will make the present era famous for architectural ugliness'. All the new housing was brick with tile or slate roofs. The *Chronicle* in July 1901 congratulated Dorchester because 'over the last ten or twenty years the town has come into favour as a

89 Fordington from the meadows, showing the density of houses and terraces which had developed in the small area available for housing. Dorchester's churches are clearly seen on the right.

73

90 Mill Street, Fordington about 1900, then notorious slums, and the most densely populated part of Dorchester. All the thatched cottages were later demolished during slum clearance.

desirable residential place ... The erection of many commodious and elegant villas' and the creation of the Borough Gardens, along with improved drainage, had made the town grow.

The enclosure of Fordington led to the need for children's play areas. In the late 19th century the walls were defended by a keeper who was there to repel children and stop them from climbing the trees. Since he was usually old and the walks extensive it was easy for children to evade him. The Borough Gardens had a children's playground at the south end when it opened in 1895, but only five years later the bowling green and tennis courts were constructed in its place. By 1913 there were complaints that there was nowhere for Dorchester children to play: 'The

91 Cornhill about 1910, with the traffic still two-way. South Street was becoming the main shopping street.

rich man with his motor has annexed the country roads, making them almost impossible for a quiet stroll and extremely dangerous to children.' Children were not allowed to play in the Borough Gardens, so they 'have to content with the rough gravel walks and come home with cut knees'. 'The grass plots may only be used for bowlers, tennis players and their friends ... If a lady and her little girl sit under the shade of a tree on a Saturday, where the friends of tennis players may make themselves comfortable on a week-day, they are politely warned by the gardeners that they "must come off the grass"'. (Letters to the *Dorset County Chronicle*, June 1913).

Hardy's Casterbridge started to become a tourist attraction from about 1900. People wanted to see the places made famous by Hardy's novels, and were looking for colourful rural nostalgia. Arthur Tomson, visiting in 1901, was typical in his focus:

Time, fire and even worse enemy than either of these—the jerry-builder—have been by no means merciful to Dorchester ... Possibly in no other part of the kingdom exists any place that tells quite so clearly of the occupation of those who reside in its immediate neighbourhood. Villa may be added to villa; wing after wing of new buildings may be shot out from the ancient enclosure into the surrounding hills, and yet Dorchester remains obviously the centre, the place of business of a peculiarly rural population.

It is, of course, on market days and on fair days that this delightful characteristic is to be felt most keenly. From early morning, on such days, to the bugle calls from the barracks, to the rattle of an occasionally hurrying cart—sounds that usually break the calm of Dorchester streets—are added the bleating of sheep, the lowing of cows, and the more peevish and impetuous cries of numberless

92 The south end of South Street about 1920, with Napper's Mite and its useful clock left.

have brought forth from the very depths of their stores merchandise that intrudes far upon the public footway. And what a charm there is about the peculiar products of the shops in a really agricultural neighbourhood! I do not refer to the clothes they offer, nor the books, nor any of the elegancies of life; such things can be viewed, at all events in greater profusion, in London. The shops that really satisfy one are those that supply agriculture instruments of every kind, all sorts of horse garniture, seeds, manures, baskets large and small, and of every device and shape, and everything, in fact, that has about it, however remotely, the distinct poetry of outdoor life. Not only are the suggestions arising from these wares healthy and inspiring, but about the very make of the pieces of handicraft there is an honesty and a beauty too often wanting in the things manufactured principally for town people. Even in a garden wheel-barrow, for instance, there are forms more graceful and more worthy than may be found in many an 'art-Chair' created by some advertised London firm.

Not by any means to be missed are the sales by auction, commencing in the market place about noon. Here one may study character and dialect; inquire into various characteristics of different sorts of beasts, and be amused by the resourceful speech of the auctioneers; and full well must he have feasted in wonders, who can regard unmoved so many cheeses, so many eggs, so many farm cattle, so many tokens of the unfailing industry of man, and bird, and beast.

Dorchester wanted to be seen as up-to-date but, as ever, many visitors were attracted by the old world, rural and backward. This was to be a problem for the town right through the 20th century.

Most of the shops and other businesses had been in the High Streets, the main through route for roads, but the railways had altered this; South Street was the entrance to the town from both stations, and shops started to open along what had been a residential street. In their customary round-up of the shops in Dorchester at Christmas 1901, the *Chronicle* emphasised that it had to be brief, 'for the number of shops in Dorchester has so increased of late years with the growing reputation of the Borough as a business town, and the individual proprietors have so bestirred them-selves to "keep pace with the times" that it is

calves. For miles around, on all the roads that lead to Dorchester, the sheep may be seen moving slowly, and in dry weather in dense clouds of dust.

By mid-day all within the town is a scene of genial activity. Men—healthy, shrewd, kindly-faced men—may be seen moving about in every direction; not with the nervous restlessness of the city man, but with the rapidity that comes from bodily strength rather than anxiety. Whole families may be seen exchanging salutations at the street corners, or anywhere about the pavement or roadways; in the roadways, too – the farmer loves an open space - a great deal of preliminary business is transacted. The shopkeepers, having found their windows inadequate for the display of their wares,

93 & **94** These two views of South Street show the changes between 1860 (top) and 1910. South Street was residential in 1860, and by 1910 full of offices such as the Post Office (left, built 1906) and shops.

95 Higgins, High East Street, a typical butcher's shop about 1900.

impossible for the newspaper to describe them all'. (They would like to because they wanted the advertising next year.)

Shops were continually changing and up-dating themselves, although it is difficult to appreciate the alterations today because of more recent and much more sweeping changes. When in 1913 W.H. Smith opened their new 'Literature Depot' at 8 South Street the *Dorset County Chronicle* was impressed by the fact that the new shop was set back two feet from the frontage, so that customers were 'free from the jostling of passers by' when they admired the windows, and for the first time in Dorchester there was 'a convenient bookstall window, at which one can be served promptly with a daily paper or an

illustrated magazine without taking the time and trouble to enter the shop'.

Dorchester had always been the county town, but until the establishment of the county councils in 1889 the county administration merely comprised four meetings a year of the county justices in Shire Hall (which was also the court). Until the 1860s they looked after bridges and the one county prison (in Dorchester). Then they added the county police and the lunatic asylum. As their functions increased they expanded from Shire Hall and the Judge's House next door into Stratton Manor (purchased 1909) and by 1938 they were in six different buildings in Dorchester. The county had bought Colliton Park in the 1920s, and the foundation stone for the new

96   The entrance to the Barracks and Bridport Road about 1905. Soldiers sit on a bench by the keep, and Dorchester tradesmen pose for the photographer.

97   County Hall, Colliton Park from the air in the later 1950s. The County Council has been a major employer in Dorchester since the 1920s. The new County Hall was started in September 1938, the original plans for a stone-faced building being abandoned in order to save money. Delays caused by the Second World War delayed completion until 1955.

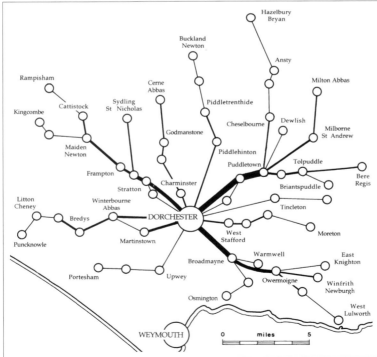

98 Mr Pitcher, a carrier from Litton Cheney, in High West Street in 1899. He was one of three carriers working from Litton Cheney: all came to Dorchester on Saturdays. The horse-drawn carriers' vans were sometimes quite small, as here: others were larger and had two horses.

99 The routes of the carriers from the 1911 *Directory*. The carriers were based in the villages, and came into Dorchester usually on Wednesdays and Saturdays. Virtually every village had at least one carrier. The train had replaced all the Weymouth carriers, but other places on the railways such as Maiden Newton had both trains and carriers. (Map by Christopher Chaplin.)

100 Eldridge Pope's brewery was the largest industrial building in Dorchester, constructed in the 1880s. By 1900 they were one of the largest employers in the town.

County Hall was laid in September 1938. Completion was delayed by the Second World War, and the final part (the Crown Court) was not finished until 1955.

In 1910 Hardy complained that 'like all other provincial towns, [Dorchester] will lose its individuality—has lost much of it already. We have become a London suburb, owing to quick locomotion'.

The coaches (and later the railways) were important for longer distance transport, and from about 1800 Dorchester was also linked to its hinterland by regular carrier vans which ran into the town on specific days. The 1840 *Directory* shows what these services were like before the railways came: of 14 carriers listed, there were two to London or Poole, three to Bristol and four to Weymouth. Beaminster and Bridport are the only other destinations. These long-distance carriers were superseded by the railways, but in 1880 there were still 42 local carriers working into Dorchester from as far afield as Blandford and Hazelbury Bryan.

The Blandford service ran every day, but the Hazelbury one was only on Saturday, the main market day. Most of the carriers came on Wednesday and Saturday, the market days, bringing in passengers and orders for goods from the villages. Mrs. Legg remembered Puddletown in 1900: 'Carrier Caundle went to Dorchester at 10 a.m. daily, first he would go round the village and collect orders, he would bring back anything, fish or meat for dinner, or Goulds would send out a large box of hats or underwear, Frisby's big parcels of shoes' on approval for people to choose from and then pay. He started back from Dorchester at 4 p.m., putting his van and horses up at the *White Hart*, the very first public house on the road in from Puddletown.

Hardy used one of the local carrier's vans from the *White Hart* as the vehicle for a series of short stories called 'A Few Crusted Characters' published in 1891. 'These vans, so numerous hearabouts, are a respectable, if somewhat lumbering, class of conveyance, much resorted to by decent travellers not overstocked with money.' Half an hour before the carrier's leaving time, 'errand boys from the shops begin to arrive with packages, which they fling into the vehicle, and turn away whistling', then the passengers start to arrive, and sit in the van even though the horse has yet to be put in the shafts.

101 Eldridge Pope's huge maltings, built in the 1870s between Charles Street and Acland Road, photographed just before their demolition in the 1960s.

102 Lott & Walne's Foundry was an important part of Edwardian Dorchester, producing water-carts for watering the streets to keep the dust down (seen here outside the foundry), ploughs, horse shoes and rollers, and shepherds' huts on wheels. They also made and installed pumps on wells for water supplies. They continued casting metals into the 1960s. The premises are now flats.

In 1901 the police decided that carriers' vans were obstructions in the streets. Their horses were stabled at the various inns and public houses, but there was not enough room for the vans themselves on Wednesdays and Saturdays, so they were left in the streets as they had been for many years. Thirty-seven of the carriers petitioned the Town Council to be allowed to use the streets as they had always done, reminding the Council that 'they were indirectly the means of spending a lot of money in Dorchester'. The council agreed: 'Dorchester was chiefly a trading town, and the majority of them had to live out of what they could get from their neighbours and people coming from the country districts. These vans were a means of bringing buyer and seller together, and a great convenience both to the tradesmen in the town and the residents in the country districts.' Happily, the carriers and the Council won the battle with the police, and the carriers' vans kept coming.

The peak of their activity was the late 19th-century years and up to the First World War, when more than forty different carriers ran services into Dorchester. After the First World War some carriers changed to motorised small buses, and by 1923 the *Directory* could state that most of the carriers now used motor vehicles. Their trade was being affected by the new 'Motor Omnibus Service' which was running to Weymouth and Bridport several times each day.

Some of the carriers developed into bus or coach services themselves, and by 1938 there were only 28 carriers left. However, because the motor buses were so much quicker, many were offering two or even three trips a day, and stating their travel times (whereas beforehand the day alone had been sufficient because horse-drawn vans would leave the villages in the morning and return in the late afternoon). In 1938 more than half the carriers were using the Council Yard in Trinity Street as their Dorchester depot: the buses didn't need stables.

Industry also developed on the newly enclosed land. The largest employer was Eldridge Pope's brewery which opened in 1881 next to the railway on what had been part of Fordington fields. This was rail-served, as was Eddison's Steam Plough Works further east. The town never developed enough industry: in 1900 the Corporation was complaining that what was needed was 'some good factories to provide employment for young women'. The 1903 *Directory* listing most of the trades in the town includes many craftsmen of a type which would have been found in the town from much earlier days: blacksmiths, boot-makers, milliners, dairymen, wheelwrights, basket makers, tailors, coach builders, a bath chairman, painters, grocers and many other sorts of shopkeepers. Amongst them are signs of the future: two electrical engineers, one garage, one typist and a petroleum merchant.

Nine

The Victorian Legacy

The Victorians gave Dorchester many buildings which still survive, but they also left a less physical legacy of services and institutions, many of which we take for granted. These include clean water, sewers, gas and other powers; telegraph and telephone; universal schooling; police and even the idea of public lavatories.

After the demise of the Roman aqueduct Dorchester's water came from wells or the river. The town pump in the middle of South Street, erected in 1784, was an attempt at a public supply, a more elegant successor to a public well of the medieval period which was further down South Street. In 1852 the General Board of Health was called in because the average mortality for the seven years from 1844 exceeded 23 per 1,000, the level at which their interference was warranted. Their report proved that all the well and pump water in Dorchester was contaminated,

103 The Dorchester Steam Laundry from a 1920s advertisement, with one of their delivery vehicles parked outside. Parts of the buildings survive on Bridport Road incorporated in a garage.

mostly with sewage. Only cess pits were used, some of which were only emptied once in three years. They recommended a proper water works and sewers.

These recommendations were accepted, but not without strong opposition from Rev. Henry Moule. He had developed a system of using dry sifted earth 'for the removal and utilisation of excrementious matter'. In 1862 he patented his earth closet, which 'flushed' one pint of earth per use. Thousands were sold to prisons, barracks and even Queens' College Cambridge. They went on being produced into the 20th century, but Moule could not convince local or national government that it was the right system for towns and cities. The earth was dried after use (it was claimed with no smell at all) and then sold as manure. Moule claimed that the 'vast and extravagant works for public drainage added 6d. a week to the rent of the cottage of the mechanic or labourer' in Dorchester, while 'the earth system, fully and fairly carried out, would have increased his income'.

The General Board of Health recommended that Whitwell Spring, at the foot of Poundbury, which 'had long been resorted to by some of the inhabitants of Dorchester as 'having certain medicinal qualities', and also made better tea than pump water, should be used for the public supply, with a covered reservoir on the summit of Poundbury. The engineer entrusted with the works could not get the consent of all those claiming part of the water from the spring, so he had a deep well dug up the Bridport Road (where the water-works still are) and the water raised by steam engine to a covered reservoir. Thirty thousand feet of water mains were laid at a cost of £4,300. Water rates were meant to be 2d. a week per house supplied. The same engineer planned the sewers for Dorchester, which cost £4,000. He had human manure analysed, and it was found to be 'more valuable than farmyard dung' but not as good as

104 One of Dorchester's gas lamps in High West Street, photographed about 1860. They cost as much as £160 a year in gas but were, according to the Board of Health Report of 1852, justified because 'in a town lamps take the place of police, and *prevent* much immorality and crime'.

Peruvian guano. The engineer decided that the Corporation should not build a sewage works, but leave it to a 'responsible party who might be willing to rent the sewerage and to turn it to his own profit'. He used a 'natural outfall' below Loud's Mill, so the £4,000 worth of sewers simply shot all the sewage into the river.

This continued until 1899 when the Corporation built the first sewage farm on the current site, and were then sued by the occupant of a nearby house because the smells were so awful. During the court case one judge sarcastically remarked that 'ultimately, even the Corporation began to think that [putting the sewage straight into the river] was not altogether an entirely satisfactory mode'.

A characteristic Victorian enterprise combining cleanliness with money making was the Dorchester Steam Laundry, which was built close to the waterworks in 1879 and cost nearly as much—£3,000. In *Views and Reviews* (1898) the improvement in hygiene is extolled: 'impossible in the day of the peggy-tub and the widowed washerwoman'. The Steam Laundry offered 'thorough hygiene and efficiency ... occupying an elevated position on the outskirts of the Borough ... well removed from the town smoke. The only detergents requisitioned are high pressure steam and the best superfatted soap ... The establishment is noted for the uniform excellence and superior finish of its starched work and also for the promptitude and punctuality with which goods are returned to their owners.'

Public lavatories, available to people of all classes, did not exist until 1851, when a pioneer built 'retiring rooms' at the Great Exhibition in

105 Dorchester Gasworks from the air, probably in the 1920s. The two gasometers are clear. Unlike later 19th-century industries, the gasworks ignores the railway because it predates it.

106 Advertisement for the Electrical Exhibition in May 1926: poor timing as it coincided with the General Strike and there wasn't enough electricity to run the appliances all the time. The Corn Exchange was not yet fitted with electricity, so supply came from a 'feeder pillar' in the road outside. On the left is a 'bungalow cooker' (which cost £5 12s.), and the extraordinary device on the right is a fire. 'By means of electricity it is possible to have a cheerful, radiant fire in any room at any hour, without labour before or after use.' Centre right is a washing machine, and the earphones were for the wireless. A valve crystal set cost £5 and a three-valve Marconi a staggering £25. Some of the most popular items were the electrical pumps for wells.

the face of considerable opposition. They were slow to spread: by 1895 just 36 towns had public lavatories. Many of them were underground, like Dorchester's first at the end of South Street. There were many objections when these were proposed in 1913: 'it was most objectionable. It would be an awful nuisance to see people going in and out of the proposed convenience' stated a middle-class neighbour, but they were built underground that they 'might not be offensive to the eye'.

Up to the early 19th century water, horses and people were the only sources of power. The river was harnessed for watermills, which ground corn and fulled cloth, and horses were used for all transport. From the 1830s early steam engines were being used for industry.

Dorchester's gasworks opened in 1833, and was extolled by the *Chronicle* as 'one of the greatest improvements ever affected in this town'. When 'the lamps in the public streets, in the shops, and in private houses [were] lighted, a blaze of brilliancy was cast over the town'. Dorchester considered its new gas to be 'of superior brilliancy and purity' which helped to make the light brighter, and the town had extravagantly placed the street lamps 'more closely together than in almost every other town'. Together these made the town very light.

Almost all the shops were lit by gas as well as a few private houses, though some refused to have it, fearing that it would prove unsafe. The gasworks cost £4,000 which included £10 4s. for a dinner for the 68 men who built it. By 1852 there were 72 public lamps lit by gas, all in the town itself, none in Fordington. They were lit for 10 months of the year from sunset to sunrise, except for an economical five nights around each full moon. In 1840 there were 360 'private lights' and in 1851 this had increased to 1,650. Gas was then virtually only used for lighting.

By the 1890s efficient gas cookers and fires were available, and the demand for gas increased rapidly. The peak of production for the Dorchester works was in 1946 and the very cold year 1947, when 137 and 148 million cubic feet of gas was sold. In one day in January 1947, 701,000 cubic feet of gas was sent out from the works. In March 1949 the local company was nationalised, and became part of the Southern Gas Board. The town had a gasworks from about the same date as most other places, but it was late in getting electricity. The *King's Arms* was the

earliest building in the town to have electric lighting, in 1889, from a private supply powered by the steam engines in the Aerated Waterworks (making minerals) at the back of the hotel. Dynamos were fitted to supply enough electricity for 20 lamps, which were mostly in the 'wine and spirit vaults where their superior light has been generally noticed'. The *King's Arms* hoped to extend the system 'on a larger scale and more economically'.

Channons coach factory installed its own system in 1901, with a large 'electric arc lamp of 1,200 candle power' out in the street, and lamps in all the workshops. A gas engine was used to generate power, and there was no battery storage, 'Mr Channon preferring to use his electricity as he makes it'. The ease of use impressed the *Chronicle*'s reporter: the electric lights 'can be used in any one room separately if it is desired, as there are in each room the means of turning it on and off'. The novelty of switches: for gas lighting one had to turn a tap and then light the gas.

A public electricity supply was proposed from 1900 but wasn't really started until 1906 when a private company, the Dorchester Electric Light and Power Company, was established. The Borough took over the company in 1922, when it could produce just 125 kilowatts from its plant in Church Street. By 1926 the Borough had increased output to 520 kilowatts, still very small. In 1927 the Dorn Electrical Company fitted up a new bungalow in Coburg Road as an all-electric home and opened it as an advertisement. All the lighting and heating were electric, as well as the cooker. An electric kettle, vacuum sweeper, boiler, hair dryer and iron were used, but the three items which caused the most interest were an electric warming pad for feet or body with three different temperatures possible, an ultra-violet (or artificial sunlight, as it was then called) radiation treatment machine, and the 'self-contained larder' or refrigerator which cost £30. The electricity supply did not run as far as Coburg Road, so a small power plant had to be installed to run the equipment.

The telegraph was the first reliable and quick long-distance communicator, memorably described recently as the Victorian Internet. From 1845 messages could be sent instantaneously across the country. The system of necessary wires was generally run alongside the railway lines which

107 Dorchester's first telephone exchange at Cedar Court Villas, Trinity Street.

were being constructed at just the time telegraphy was also expanding. In 1852 a large advertisement in the *Chronicle* announced that the Electric Telegraph Company had opened an office at Dorchester railway station, and messages of 20 words could be sent to London or anywhere within 100 miles for 2s. 6d. More than 100 miles cost 5s. Dorchester's telegrams were dealt with by the Post Office from the early 1870s, with the office open the same hours, but 'messages may be sent at any hour of the night or day by paying an additional fee' (*Directory of Dorsetshire Towns*, 1874/5).

The first place in Dorchester to have a telephone was the post office. In March 1878 the *Chronicle*'s reporter was invited to witness a 'telephonic interview' between Dorchester and Puddletown post offices 'and could not but be surprised at what took place'. A conversation was heard 'with the greatest distinctness' and Puddletown also obliged by singing 'Out in the Green Fields'. Dorchester reciprocated with the less folksy 'Tiddly-wink' and tunes on the harmonium were returned from Puddletown. The Post Office telephones were part of the telegraphic service, for internal use only, and from 1907 the Post Office impressively described itself as a 'Telephonic Express Delivery Office'.

The *King's Arms* had the first private line in Dorchester, and was connected to the Weymouth

exchange because there was not yet one in Dorchester. The National Telephone Company opened an exchange in Dorchester in a private house in 1899, but by 1907 there are still only five telephone numbers listed in the local *Directory*; all commercial—a grocer, solicitor, printer, vet and ironmonger. In 1910 the Post Office took over all telephones, and it was the *King's Arms* rival, the *Antelope*, which became Dorchester telephone no.1. Eldridge Pope were no.2. There were still only nine subscribers listed in 1911, all commercial. By the 1923 *Kelly's Directory* Dorchester had 108 telephones in commercial premises, and three in private houses—(two of them in Queen's Avenue); the 1954 *Longman's Directory of Dorchester* has 11 pages of local telephone numbers: the *Antelope* is still simply 1, although some subscribers had four digit numbers by then.

Pre-Victorian schools in Dorchester, as elsewhere, were all for boys and mostly for the middle and upper classes. The Dorchester National School was the first to try to educate the working classes, and was established in 1812, only a year after the founding of the Society for Promoting the Education of the Poor in the Principles of the Established Church. The British & Foreign Society ran early schools which were non-sectarian and attracted many nonconformist children whose parents did not want them educated in the principles of the established church, i.e. the Church of

England. Dorchester had a British school from the 1820s, which Thomas Hardy attended from 1849 for seven years. He was nine when he started: a typical pattern as the villages could only supply a simple education for younger children who had to come into the towns for anything more.

Dorchester had its old grammar school, and in the 19th century many schools of different types were established, so that by 1852 there were 14, four of them boarding schools and three supported by the government for the education of the poor. Some were quite small. The Rev. Henry Moule in Fordington educated boys at his home, and William Barnes ran a school in South Street for 27 years from 1835. In his last year, one of his pupils came top for the entire country in the examinations for the Indian Civil Service. Ironically his school had been failing, with the numbers falling, but because of this success he was besieged with applications. Barnes dryly pointed out that 'it took two to do it'.

From medieval times the Borough paid for local constables to keep the town in order, but by the early 19th century they had been reduced to watchmen who walked the streets at night. L.C. Boswell-Stone remembered 'the watchman was a great institution in those days: besides calling the hour he always informed us of the exact state of the weather—"a thunder and lightning night" was duly reported'. An examination of the structure and personnel of the Borough in 1834, just before it was reformed, showed that three night watchmen were employed, but not every night. The two sergeants at mace told the enquiry that 'by their voluntary consent they have occasionally been sworn as special constables: otherwise they do not act as police officers'. The beadles and watchmen were not enough to keep the peace at times of tumult, such as the elections: regular soldiers had to be used as the last resort.

The Dorset Yeomanry were founded in 1794, during the Napoleonic Wars. Their first stated purpose was 'repelling insurrections at home' and 'suppression of Riots and Tumults'. Helping regular troops if the enemy invaded seems to have been an afterthought.

The Captain Swing protests in 1830 against the new threshing machines and low agricultural wages show how Dorchester (and the county) coped with riots when there were no yeomanry or police. The Yeomanry had been disbanded at the end of the Napoleonic Wars in

108 The brand new school in Victoria Park, 1911, built from Doddings Bere Regis bricks. There were five elementary schools in Dorchester in 1911: this one was for 352 girls and infants. In 1930 the secondary girls moved to a new school in Queen's Avenue.

1814, and the Borough Police were not established until 1836. The magistrates were sitting at County Hall, Dorchester (Shire Hall) when the rioting started and 'a great number of gentlemen and farmers from all the neighbouring parishes came into the town, on horseback, tendering their assistance to the magistrates, as an armed patrol, to put down any seditious assemblages, and to preserve the peace'. There were no regular soldiers quartered in the county, so the farmers and gentlemen were sworn in as special constables, to make their patrols legal. In Dorchester men on foot armed with staves guarded the town, 'one company [of 12 to 15 men] from each parish assembling nightly to patrol the town'. The magistrates, the only people who could swear in special constables, were employed full-time in doing so. A troop of regular soldiers soon arrived in Dorchester to keep the peace. These were the traditional methods of preserving the peace before there were police.

In 1835 Dorchester set up a Borough Police Force, which sounded good but was really no different from the old parish constable system. There were two night watchmen patrolling the town, and two more in Fordington. The Yeomanry had been revived after the 1830 riots, but were 'ungraciously and insolently disbanded' again in 1839. The adjectives come from the very Conservative local newspaper (*The Dorset County Chronicle*) which did not like the idea of a police

109 The Borough Police in 1889, the year they were absorbed into the County Police. The 1889 *Directory* gives the full complement as a superintendent (William Gale, centre) two sergeants (seated) and five constables (six in the photograph). Like the county police of the time, all have moustaches.

force because it was controlled by central government rather than local gentry.

By the 1860s there were a few more police, but unfortunately they were not always popular of even effective.

Dorchester customarily celebrated 5 November by rolling lighted tar barrels down the handy hill of the High Streets. The lower orders of the town dressed up in grotesque costumes (which helped as no-one could identify them), rolled barrels, threw fireworks and some-times used this time of licence to protest. In 1863 the effigy paraded through the town was not Guy Fawkes, but P.C. Cosens of the Borough Police. In the next year's celebrations Cosens felled a man letting off fireworks with such force that his staff broke in two. The crowd turned on him and 'the police had to beat a hasty retreat into the Town Hall'. The crowd 'swearing vengeance on the offending officer and his colleagues' threw stones at the Town Hall and the Borough Police station behind, and 'then there were cries of "Out with the Bobbies" and an assault was made on the doors of the hall, which only just held'. All the windows were broken. The *Dorset County Chronicle* admitted that Cosens had 'lost his tem-per, and if anything exceeded the bounds of prudence'. The newspaper thought it was 'useless

to attempt to put down these demonstrations with such a handful of men as constitute the police force of this borough'.

Four days later Cosen's effigy was again paraded through the streets 'followed by about 2,000 persons, yelling and shouting—composed mostly of females' and then it was burnt in Maumbury Rings. Five days later this was re-peated, the effigy this time being decapitated at Maumbury. The Borough enlisted many special constables to deal with the disturbances, and one man refused to serve partly because he would not take an oath, but mostly because 'I feel I could not take a staff and knock people down as I am required to do', a cynical but truthful view of service as a special constable. The town had apparently recruited 200 special constables to deal with the protests, using them as they had used the military, especially the Yeomanry in the past. Clearly the Borough Police could be individually unbelievably unpopular, and there were not enough of them to control any riots.

The Borough Police were merged with the County Police in 1889, and started to become more like a modern force. The County Police Station had been built tactfully on what was then the outskirts of the town in 1860, four years after the county force was set up.

Ten

The First World War

Dorchester was a military town, well used to soldiers in its streets and the call of the bugle from the barracks off Bridport Road, but the First World War filled the town with the military, both native and German. In August 1914, just after the start of the war, Hardy wrote, 'Dorchester is teeming with soldiers, mostly drunk'.

The town was receiving German prisoners less than two weeks after the outbreak of hostilities, housing them in the old artillery barracks of Poundbury Road. The earliest arrivals were German seamen caught in harbour by the outbreak of war, and interned Austrian and German civilians. By the end of August there were 1,000 prisoners, many of them soldiers, and Hardy wrote of 'sentries with gleaming bayonets at unexpected places, and the 1,000 prisoners whom we get glimpses of through chinks … the prisoners, they say, have already mustered enough English to say "Shoot Kaiser" and oblige by playing "God Save the King" on their concertinas and fiddles. Whether this is "meant sarcastic", I cannot tell.'

By the end of 1914 there were so many prisoners that huts were erected near the barracks to accommodate them, and afterwards the camp expanded up the hillside to the banks of Poundbury Iron-Age hill-fort. The International

110   Some of the earliest German prisoners-of-war being marched off after arriving at Dorchester by train, probably August 1914. Crowds of people went to see them arrive.

111 At Channons during the First World War. The garage made parts for gun carriages and was one of the earliest in the area to employ women. Edward Channon is seated centre in a hat, his son Ernest on his left and Ernest's wife second from left. Channons seems to have been the only war production in Dorchester, but many people supplied goods to the soldiers and prisoners.

Red Cross inspected the camp in January 1915 when it held 1,000 prisoners, one-tenth of the 10,000 in the whole country, and found it a model one, both the barracks and the huts being lit by electricity and heated by coal stoves. Each man was well-dressed, bathed daily, and had plenty of food. They went out for long walks, suitably guarded, and many worked inside the camp, as tailors, shoemakers or on the building of the huts and roads, for small wages. By the end of 1915 there were 3,500 prisoners, and a German-speaking reporter who visited found the only complaint was the lack of black bread; the Commandant was trying to obtain rye flour so that it could be provided.

Dorchester folk found the prisoners-of-war fascinating, getting as close to the camp as they could to look at them, but they soon stopped meeting every group as it arrived at the railway station, as they had done at first. Women loitering in the neighbourhood of the camp were a problem in 1915: they had 'communicated with the im-prisoned officers by nods and the throwing of kisses'. The newspaper reported ominously that their identities were known. By late 1916 there were 5,000 prisoners so there was virtually a second, satellite town run on German lines by the prisoners themselves. Dorchester itself only had 9,000 people at this time, so there were more males in the prison camp than there were in the town itself. The prisoners were not repatriated until November 1919, and they provided a great deal of useful manpower, working on the farms, sweeping the streets,

112 Inside Boon's, the grocers, in 1907. The four assistants are all men; this would change in the First World War.

quarrying gravel and sand, and even being hired out. Hardy employed some to cut the roots away from trees at Max Gate in 1917, paying 6d. an hour, of which the prisoners only received 1d. He noted that 'thousands of these prisoners are craving agricultural work instead of idleness, but cannot get it'. Alfred Pope complained that the Bridport Road avenue of trees (now gone) was spoilt after the Borough used German prisoners to 'ruthlessly pollard' half of them.

The main barracks were full of soldiers all through the war, and there was also a large tented camp for regular soldiers at South Court estate in 1914-15 and a smaller one for the prison guards at Poundbury. In July 1915 Hardy wrote, 'We have a large cavalry camp here, and hear the reveillé sounded at 5 in the morning.

We have also foot: so the town is sometimes a surging mass of soldiers.' Servicemen were also billeted on the town: in February 1915 men of the Royal Naval Division were accommodated in the Town Hall, where 'large quantities of straw were strewn on the floors' for them to sleep on. There were others in the Conservative Club and Duke's Salesroom. The prisoner-of-war camp had a hospital, as did the barracks, and there were two other hospitals in the town as well as the County Hospital. Colliton Park was a large military hospital from November 1914 to May 1919; there were 200 beds, and 2,000 wounded men from France were treated there. A smaller hospital in Church Street had room for only 16 patients and was open for two years from October 1914.

113 The Soldiers' Home, North Square, established in 1885 as a coffee bar and reading room to tempt soldiers out of the pubs. It was especially busy in the First World War, when this photograph was taken.

The war changed many women's lives. As the 1923 Dorchester *Official Guide* noted, 'It is a fundamental truism that a woman's place is in the home, but the cataclysm of 1914-18 effectively disproved of the common assumption that the activities of wife or daughter were limited to the confines made by the four walls of a dwelling house. Today, in the new-found emancipation of women, the prudery and prejudice of Victorian days has been trodden underfoot.' In October 1918 Hardy wrote in a letter, 'If I were a woman, I should think twice before entering into matrimony in these days of emancipation, when everything is open to the sex.' The war opened up opportunities for women simply because with so many men in the forces there was such a huge demand for labour. More than 1,500 men from Dorchester served during the war, and in 1918 the Mill Street Mission stated that 'from the 161

houses which the Mission considers its parish, between 300 and 350 men and boys' had joined the forces. Fordington houses were very crowded, but nevertheless this gives some idea of the numbers who fought.

Fifty-one Dorchester women and girls worked as VAD (Voluntary Aid Detachment) in the hospitals, particularly Colliton Hospital. Many of them were middle class, and before the war they would not have expected to work at all. Shop assistants in 1914 were virtually all male, but gradually they were replaced by women. The Post Office shocked Dorchester by employing women letter-carriers (somehow not postwomen) from 1915. 'To some people the innovation has its humorous aspect', noted the *Chronicle*. These were working-class women, but in 1916 Dorchester appointed a 'lady head postman' whom the newspaper carefully pointed out

114   One of the 'grand procession of over 25 decorated motor cars, representing the British Empire, our Forces, and our Allies' which was the most exciting part of Kut Day, July 1916, organised to raise money to send comforts to 370 Dorset soldiers who became prisoners of the Turks after the siege at Kut-el-Almra. O.C. Vidler's car, seen here in the barracks, represented France, with Kathleen, his daughter, standing in the back.

was the daughter of a local sergeant-major. In January 1917 the *Chronicle* visited the Dorchester Post Office to see how the women had coped with the Christmas mail rush (increased greatly by the prisoner-of-war camp, which received 1,500 parcels at Christmas 1914 when there were only 1,000 prisoners; by 1917 there were 5,000). The reporter found that 'at present women are doing all telegraph operating and counter work, and also the bulk of the duty in the sorting office, and the outdoor deliveries. Indeed, at present the Post Office is almost a woman-con-trolled establishment. Moreover', showing how the war had speeded things up, 'after only a few weeks of experience the women are now doing, and doing efficiently, work for which in peace time men used to undergo two or three years of training.'

By 1915 shop hours were being curtailed. Until then shops opened early and stayed open until 9 or 9.30p.m., later on Saturdays. Some shops started closing at 7p.m., and some at 6p.m., except for Saturdays, and soon afterwards they

started closing for a dinner hour from 1.15 to 2.15p.m. Women worked at Channon's garage making parts for gun carriages, and they were also encouraged to work on the land as more and more labourers were called up. The Women's Land Army was exactly like its better known Second World War equivalent. By January 1918 there were 1,100 women working on Dorsetshire farms, and 250 of them marched through Dorchester to a rally. The *Chronicle* was a bit shocked that they had 'doffed the conventional skirt so long associated with their sex', but admitted that 'many of them wore their breeches and gaiters, picturesque smocks and jaunty hats with a delightful touch of piquancy and the chic so valued by the fair'. 'Gazing at their robust yet supple figures and observing the sparkle of their eyes and the bloom of their well-moulded cheeks one could have no shadow of doubt that the open-air life and healthy labour has done them a world of good … Here is dawning a new era for womanhood, and therefore for the human race!'

115   The VAD Hospital in Colliton Park with wounded soldiers and nurses. The hospital overflowed into marquees in the grounds: the wooden shelters were sometimes used for patients to sleep in, an approved treatment for TB or gassing.

116   The old house at Colliton being used as a hospital in the First World War. The roofs cover corridors between the house and the marquees.

117 Poundbury prisoner-of-war camp being extended, probably in 1916. The tents were for the prison guards. The hill-fort of Poundbury is just visible centre: it was used as an exercise yard, with guards patrolling on the ramparts.

The First World War also had its Home Guard; Dorchester was one of the earliest places to establish a Volunteer Corps for Home Defence, in December 1914. They soon gained 100 members, which in 1916 increased to 200. They were not officially approved of until later in 1916, and so had to raise the money for arms and uniforms themselves. After 1916 they even had machine-gun units, and all the Volunteers, who were mostly over military age or in reserved occupations, trained several times a week. The officers were mostly local tradesmen and professional people, not the gentry.

Dorchester also had a black-out. London and a few other towns had been bombed from airships, so precautions were taken from early 1915. Many street lamps were left unlit 'to break up the distinctive parallel lines of light which reveal streets to observers in hostile air-craft', and all shop lights were banned. The *Chronicle* thought the town looked as it must have done in the past, when it was lit 'with the old oil lamps, and shops were comparatively few and far between'. A local poet wrote:

> Dorchester be-nighted
> How dimly is she lighted
> Yet are we now affrighted
> By German aeroplane?

Hardy complained in a letter that he had banged himself 'against some railings in Dorchester High Street the other night - where it is as dark as a cave'. Eddison's hooter (normally used only to signal work times) was to be used as an air-raid alarm, 'blowing long and short blasts alternately for a considerable time'. It was never needed.

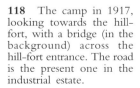

118 The camp in 1917, looking towards the hill-fort, with a bridge (in the background) across the hill-fort entrance. The road is the present one in the industrial estate.

Eleven

Between the Wars: 1920s and '30s

'You would find Dorchester externally much as it was, but considerably changed mentally—perhaps because strangers have settled it and near it ... It is pathetic enough to see on the shutters of some of the one-man shops, "Closed till the end of the war".' (Thomas Hardy, July 1918) Many people had come to the town in the war and 1,500 local men from a population of 9,000 had served in the forces; 237 of them died. A soldier who returned home to Dorchester after the war has recorded how he found everything changed. On Saturday night the streets were now deserted, whereas before the war North Square, South Street and both High Streets were thronged with busy shoppers until late in the evening. Shop assistants were not working the ludicrously long

119 The unveiling of the Dorchester Cenotaph, on Empire Day 1921. The 17-ton Portland stone block commemorated the 237 men from Dorchester who died in the war. Relatives of the casualties were in the front ranks at the ceremony, so the people on the right had all lost someone. They hold wreaths to lay on the cenotaph. Two chestnut trees of the South Walks avenue had to be felled to accommodate the memorial. During the address after the unveiling it was said that the cenotaph was not beautiful, 'and perhaps it was chosen for that very purpose, to help all who look on it to realise more fully the hideousness of war'. The nurses (background left) were from the Colliton Hospital.

120 A new detached house for sale in Dorchester for £1,200, and a pair of semi–detached houses costing £1,250 the pair, both in 1926. Most 1920s houses in Dorchester are of similar style, simpler than their Victorian and Edwardian forebears, but with the same plan. Oddly, the detached house seems to have no chimneys.

hours they had, and people's shopping habits had changed.

Dorchester Peace celebrations in July 1919 were the largest carnival the town had ever seen— led by a detachment of Dorset Yeomanry on their horses, and with a tank following the rear of the procession. The old and the new had both been important in the war. In between were 25 cars, lorries and motor cycles decorated with mostly patriotic themes. A detachment of the Women's Land Army was accompanied by a tractor driven by a woman, and one of the humorous tableaux was only too accurate in forecasting the future: it was called 'looking for a home'. The Agricultural Labourers' Union held a demonstration at Dorchester at the same time as the Peace Day procession. The Union had

gained 600 members in Dorset in June 1919 alone. They also processed, and held three meetings in the Town Hall, each of which was packed. A local speaker said that 'the people who produced the food for the country should have at least a living wage, better houses to live in, more recreation and better education for their children'. Profiteering at the expense of the working classes was condemned, and there were demands for council housing. They felt the day was not far off when Dorset would return a Labour member to Parliament.

In November 1918 the Borough was already selecting land for 'the erection of houses for the Working Classes', but the first council houses were not finished until March 1922, in Ackerman Road off Alington Avenue. All through the '20s

121 Dorchester Wireless Station, Bridport Road, about 1930. This was built in 1927, and was one of only two transmitters in the country for beam wireless. The masts were 227 feet high, and in 1930 were used for transmissions to America, Egypt, the Far East and South America. The station finally closed in 1979 because satellites had taken over. The buildings survive as a printers.

122 The most spectacular new shop in Dorchester between the wars was Thurman's in South Street, built in 1932. The tiles on the front and roof were bright blue and the window frames were stainless steel. This gorgeous example of Art Deco was demolished in 1964.

123 Buildings in South Street being demolished in 1936 to make way for Marks & Spencer's shop. The Plaza in Trinity Street is in the background. Marks & Spencer and the huge new cinema were both part of modern Dorchester. In 1936 the *Chronicle* wrote, 'to the new generation, born into a world of war, wireless, aeroplanes, motor-cars and jazz, South Street would be unrecognisable without its streamlined saloons and striking shop windows'.

and '30s the Borough was building, largely in Victoria Park, completing between 11 (1928) and 28 (1931) houses each year. From 1927, smaller houses (then called non-parlour type) were constructed, presumably as an economy measure.

Men from both Dorchester railway stations joined the 1919 Railway Strike, the first national strike to affect the town. Many men stayed at work, but enough struck to reduce the trains to about four a day. When the first train arrived on the first day of the strike, there was 'a slight demonstration from strikers who were on the bank opposite the station'. Soldiers and police were posted in the stations. The strikers were asking for better wages, and they partially succeeded.

The influenza epidemic of 1918-19 killed many people in Dorchester as it did all over the country (more than 650 in Dorset), but the period just after the war was largely a time of great hope. The Borough reported in February 1919 that many more men would be needed in the area to 'replace the German labour at the Flax Factory, Sewage Works, Borough Gardens, and

124 Dorchester Unemployment Centre was set up in 1935, by the manager of the Labour Exchange. This was their concert party, and other postcards in the same (money-raising) series show them doing exercises, playing football, learning First Aid and making rugs. The problem of unemployment was to be cured in Dorset only by the Second World War, four years later.

upon the Road Staff of the Town Council'. They were wrong: by March 1921 they had set up an Unemployment Relief Committee and the same year the Borough was offering free Christmas dinners to the unemployed and their families. Although Dorchester did not suffer as badly as the industrial districts (or even as badly as Weymouth) there were still many unemployed all through the 1920s and '30s. The Borough set up road schemes with central government funding to give the unemployed work, similar to the scheme set up in the winter of 1838/9 when the hill of Fordington High Street was lowered by the unemployed. In December 1923 the Borough received a grant to widen the junction at Top o'Town, 'considered necessary as motor traffic has considerably increased'. They wanted to move quickly so as 'to give employment during the winter months'. Poundbury was reinstated in 1921 after having been used as a prisoner-of-war camp and many other road improvements were carried out by the unemployed.

Many of the women who had worked during the war returned to their homes afterwards, but things were not quite the same. Mrs. A. Logan became the first woman town councillor in 1919.

Miss Winifride Marsden, who had been Matron of the big VAD Hospital at Colliton Park, shows the possibilities open to women between the wars: she worked with the WI, the schools and the hospitals, which could be seen as women's work, in 1927 she became a councillor, and in 1936 Dorchester's first woman mayor.

She organised the soup kitchen run by the Women's Institute in Dorchester in the winters of 1926 and 1927. In the six months from October 1926, the winter after the General Strike, 1,850 quarts were sold (at 1d. a quart).

Few in Dorset stopped work during the General Strike, and the only ones in Dorchester were the railwaymen. Trains ceased for a few days when 128 railwaymen in Dorchester struck. The local papers at the time report very little, but it is surprising to find that there was a Dorchester Strike Committee, who held a dance at the Agricultural Workers' Hall (the old Dorford Baptist Chapel at the bottom of Fordington High Street) 'where there was a large attendance'. The Great Western Railway was the worst affected, and volunteer strike breakers helped at the West Railway station. The Dorchester Board of Guardians had a long debate,

125 The Peace Pledge Union in Maumbury Rings in 1936, the largest meeting anywhere of the anti-war organisation, with between eight and ten thousand people estimated to have attended. Many people in Dorchester were involved in anti-war and internationalist movements in the '20s and '30s.

126 Cornhill about 1938, still two-way. Improved transport, with motor vans replacing the old horse-drawn carriers' vans and many private cars, made Dorchester more accessible from the surrounding countryside.

not about whether to give dole to those who struck (which they would not) but about whether a man who was out of work because of the strikers should be eligible. One guardian claimed that 'they could not compel a man to go and break a strike'. No decision was reached, because no such victim claimed the dole in Dorchester. The railwaymen of the Great Western formed up together and marched to the station when the strike failed, a formal gesture which didn't prevent half of them being sacked. At the time of the strike agricultural labourers were trying to get their wages raised to 30s. for a 51-hour week, partly on the grounds that they were being paid less than it would cost for them and their families to be kept in Dorchester Workhouse (9s. per person per week).

Modern inventions were changing some people's lives. In the week of the General Strike there was an Electrical Exhibition in the Corn Exchange arranged by the Borough who owned the Dorchester Electricity Company. It was claimed that 'the broom and washtub are giving way to the electric suction cleaner and the washing machine', but that can hardly have been true for most families. Vacuums cleaners were £7 10s., five weeks' wages for a labourer. Radios were even more expensive: 2 valves, 14 guineas; 3 valves, £25.

In 1929 Dorset County Council stopped the road schemes which had given work to the unemployed, despite the fact that central government had given 75 per cent grants for them. In 1933 they were forced to re-start them, although some councillors thought the roads would simply be a liability because they would have to be maintained, and others thought voluntary subscriptions or tax cuts were the answer. Dorchester had more than 400 unemployed in 1933. From 1930 the Mill Street Housing Society started demolishing the old houses in Fordington and building much better

127 Looking down High West Street in July 1939 (from *The Sunday Times*). The County Council were about to move out of the buildings below Shire Hall and 'there is fear that this may mean the demolition of the old buildings and replacement by modern shops'.

new ones. Florence Hardy, the novelist's widow, was chairman. By 1934 they had built 18 new houses, and refurbished 17 old ones, and the work continued into the Second World War.

A tourist in 1928 described the town as 'rich in historical associations and in a wonderful state of preservation'. He came because of Hardy's novels 'and to see the traces of bygone civilisations which are dotted about its environs'. He found the town 'restful and quiet. Its inhabitants go about their daily work soberly and of set purpose. No noisy tram cars traverse the streets, and save for an endless processing of motor cars through the main thoroughfare which is the main artery of motor traffic between Exeter and Bournemouth, there is nothing to spoil the restful atmosphere of this typical country town'. He christened Dorchester 'Tree Town' because of

the beautiful avenues and walks. The problem of being modern and 'olde worlde' simultaneously had been a problem for Dorchester from the 1880s, and would persist.

Despite the depression there was also a great deal of private housing being built. Victoria Park, Damers Road and Bridport Road were the main areas, but building, especially in the popular semi-detached style, took place on most of the fringes of the town. The late 1920s and early '30s were the worst years of the depression, but there was a surprising amount of shop-building in Dorchester at that period too. The 1930 Town Guide records that 'during the winter of 1929/30 quite a goodly number of new and most up-to-date shop fronts have been fitted, and a considerable proportion of private property has been converted into smart shops'. The most jazzy new building was Thurman's in South Street, built in 1932 in bright Art Deco style. The blue-tiled façade was emphasised by a blue roof. Sadly, it was demolished in the 1960s. Genge's, the departmental store on the corner of Trinity Street and High West Street, steadily rebuilt their large property during the '30s, but in a much more timid neo-Georgian style. This survives, though altered very recently, but most of the shop windows of the 1930s have themselves been superseded by more recent ones.

Dorchester has had a cinema from about 1910, when the Dorchester Electric Picturedrome opened in Durngate Street, one of the first three cinemas in Dorset. In 1933 the huge ultra-modern Plaza opened in Trinity Street, and the *Chronicle* noted that 'to see such a building take the place of old houses in the course of a few months must be a source of delight to every Durnovarian'. The Plaza cost £20,000 and was one of the most modern buildings in the whole county. There was a luxurious lounge and a dainty tea-room. A 'covered way which extends practically the length of the outside wall' provided cover for those waiting for the cheaper seats.

The County Library Service was founded in 1925, and had a branch in Trinity Street from 1930. This moved to County Hall in 1948, and then to the present purpose-built library in 1966.

Dorchester's first pedestrian crossings were installed in 1936. They were not, as one might expect, in the town centre, but at Fordington Cross, Weymouth Avenue (by Edward Road) and by the railway tunnel on Bridport Road. In 1936 it was also proposed that the County Council should 'purchase or hire about 70 acres in or near Dorchester for use as a landing place for aeroplanes'. One councillor complained that 'two distinguished visitors on business to Dorchester had chartered aeroplanes' but could not land. The proposal came to nothing. The Dorchester British Legion exchanged trips with ex-prisoners-of-war from the Dorchester camp in 1937, and many of the British came back convinced that Hitler was good for Germany, and only wanted peace.

Twelve

The Second World War

Everyone was affected by the Second World War: the threat of bombing, the black-out, rationing of food and other privations were the same everywhere. Dorchester was full of soldiers again because of its being a barracks town, but in the early stages of the war civilians suffered more than soldiers, and it was suggested that the troops should be set to knitting comforters for civilians.

ARP (Air Raid Precautions) were already working in Dorchester, and the black-out was immediately applied, with no street lights and all buildings 'blacked-out' as soon as it was dark. Twelve hundred evacuee children arrived from London. Some soon returned, but 800 stayed, a much higher proportion than most places. The town was pressing on with plans for air-raid shelters; only two (in Bowling Alley Walk and in the market) were new buildings. The others were the bandstand store in the Borough Gardens, and basements or cellars in the new County Hall, Colliton Park; Genges High West Street and the County Club; a malthouse in Charles Street; *Three Mariners*, High Street, and the rifle range (underground) in Princes Street. In fact, very few bombs fell on Dorchester: one made a large hole in Trinity Street and destroyed a popular baker's shop, but no-one was killed.

The war became very real in June 1940 when the evacuation from Dunkirk of all British forces in France brought hundreds of exhausted soldiers to Dorchester. The barracks overflowed and, to relieve the food and accommodation shortage, people were asked to feed and house some of them. Soldiers were so tired that they slept on people's lawns or even in the streets.

Many people worked in Civil Defence, WVS, Red Cross, the Observer Corps or fire watching on top of their usual jobs. In May 1940 the Local Defence Volunteers (soon

128 Parsons tobacconists, Cornhill, during the Second World War, with tape criss-crossed over some of the windows to prevent flying glass.

renamed the Home Guard) was established, requiring even more part-time volunteers. *The Dorset County Chronicle* reporter went out with the Dorchester Home Guard in October 1940, when they were 200 strong.

129 The Battle of Britain seen from Icen Way, Dorchester, drawn by Kathleen Vidler on 2 August 1940. Searchlights cross on a plane in trouble and trailing smoke. Kathleen recorded that in the morning they found odd-shaped bits of metal on the front doorstep and in the garden, and hoped they were from German planes, not English ones.

For the most part they are members of the professional and sub-professional class, a few are doctors and schoolmasters; some were farm labourers; many wear ex-service ribbons. They fall, in the main, in two age groups: over-thirties, many of whom earned the right to "peace in our times" twenty years ago, and the under-twenties, some of them just out of their school OTC or cadet corps, some of them the younger sons of farmers ... To

outward appearance they are soldiers. Their clothing, and latterly even their equipment are identical, but there is a free-and-easy atmosphere about their enthusiasm that is manifest in their ultra-democratic outlook.

This later faded and the Home Guard became as stratified as the Army.

Dorchester Observer Corps' post re-used the Iron-Age defences of Poundbury hill-fort. Local

130 A Civil Defence Decontamination Squad on exercise in North Square in 1941. It was thought that coastal areas would have gas attacks when the wind was in the right direction, so everyone was issued with gas masks, and the Civil Defence learnt to deal with the numerous varieties.

men manned the post right through the war to supply information on all aircraft movements to the RAF. They were in contact with the centre at Yeovil, giving identification, height, speed and direction of every plane seen or heard. Salvage or, as we would call it today, recycling was very important in the war, with paper, bone, food (for pigs), books (for soldiers) and scrap metal all being avidly collected. The heads of big game animals, including even tigers, which had decorated the Town Hall since they had been presented by a major in the First World War fell to salvage in the Second: in 1942 the Town Council decided to send them off, but just how they were recycled is difficult to imagine.

American troops started arriving in the summer of 1943. In January 1944 there was a civic reception for them, and the Mayor of Dorchester welcomed the soldiers but claimed the children of Dorchester were disappointed. Most of their information on Americans came from films and the children had expected them to arrive 'in Wild West cowboy kit, with sombreros and six-shooters'! However, when the Americans' pockets were found to be full of chewing gum and candy, they were restored to popularity. By early 1944 there were 80,000 American troops in the county, and many of them visited Dorchester. Such large quantities of exotic young men—overpaid, over-sexed and

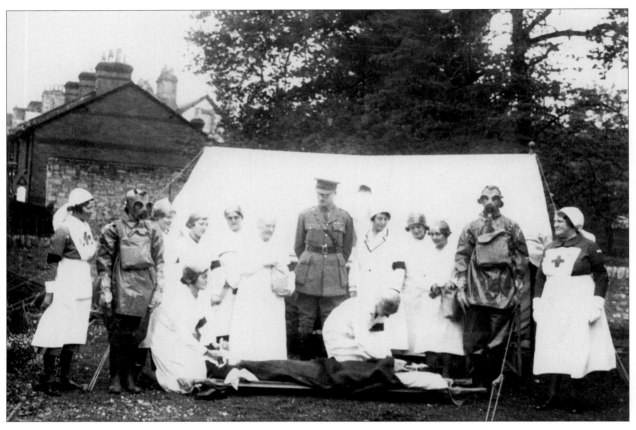

131 Dorchester First Aid Post Centre, which was manned every day in case of raids, but only by one person. Everybody has lined up for the photograph, two of them in full anti-gas gear. They were not really needed, but no-one knew where or when an air raid would take place.

over here—would have made an impression at any time, but three years into the war and with most of the local young men away in the services, they were a sensation.

They introduced baseball and American football to Dorchester in 1944, leading to long articles in the local papers attempting to explain the rules and complaining that the games were too noisy; unlike cricket, where one could get some sleep. The Americans were issued with a well-printed booklet explaining Dorset: Dorchester was 'a typical simple but dignified English county town' with an American Red Cross Club in the Corn Exchange. They were training for D-Day and, in the lead-up to embarkation, Dorchester got its first one-way system in order to deal with the huge amount of traffic. The High Streets were one way eastwards, with west-bound traffic using South Walks. South Street was one-way southwards.

Dorchester had a British Restaurant—a sort of canteen for everybody—from 1941 when the Town Council were reprimanded by central government for not having started one. It was in the front of Thurman's ironmonger's shop, next door to the Dorset County Museum, and by June 1944 it was serving 300 lunches a day. It didn't close until May 1950. There was again a prisoner-of-war camp at Dorchester, but up the Bridport Road this time. The area of the First World War prisoner camp became an Army Camp in the Second World War. The novelist Sylvia Townsend Warner, working part-time at the Dorchester WVS in July 1944, gives a vivid picture of life at the time:

132 The Women's Land Army on parade in High East Street, probably in 1943 when there were 881 land girls working on Dorset farms. Rothesay House, Dorchester was a hostel for land girls.

133   The mill at Fordington, before and after its conversion to flats in 1940. This was part of the re-housing of Fordington, and the Mill Street Mission parish magazine extolled the new building, which not only provided new homes, but improved the whole entrance to Fordington from the east.

134 German planes over Dorchester during the Second World War, photographed from the Observer Corps post on Poundbury hill-fort. The barracks entrance (now Military Museum) is clear on the centre horizon.

With the lifting of the ban we became flooded with evacuees. I spend day after day conferring with Public Assistance, Relieving Officers, Billeting Officers, WVS ladies; and hastening from one Rest Centre to another saying words of comfort such as soap flakes can be made out of solid soap by means of a cheese-grater, nobody need be ashamed of the lice nowadays, salads will not be appreciated without vinegar, Londoners seldom like porridge, pubs open at six, nettle stings are not the same as nettle-rash, fish and chips will come out in a van, lost prams shall be traced, those are *our* planes, Londoners can't be expected to go to bed before eleven, the old lady will probably leave off crying if you can get her to take her shoes off, cows don't bite, have you put up a washing-line, nursing mothers must have early morning tea, buses run on Wednesdays and Saturdays etc

The end of the war in Europe—VE Day—was celebrated in Dorchester by a combination of very local and more wide-ranging events. There were several church services and street parties were common, especially tea parties for children. North Square was typical: a tea for the children in the afternoon, with hoarded treats the long-rationed population had not seen for ages, followed by games and races, and then dancing in the flood-lit square to the music of a piano accordion and a piano up to midnight. VJ Day, when the war in the Far East was over, followed in August, and was the more dramatic: 'Soon after midnight a crowd invaded the main streets looking for material to make a Victory bonfire'. They found it in the town centre: the hoardings around the town pump, which had been used as a notice board to record War Savings, were

135 A fighter plane displayed in the Borough Gardens as part of a fund-raising exercise during the war. In July 1943 a Hurricane was displayed here as part of Wings for Victory Week, which raised £308,000, triple the target. Fund raising through War Bonds and Savings Certificates was encouraged by these special weeks.

136 Children in Orchard Street in the later 1930s, dressed up as cowboys. Until the American soldiers arrived in 1943 most people knew the United States only from films, especially cowboy films.

supplemented by display boards from the Corn Exchange. It must have been the first bonfire in the centre of the town for a long time.

Eighty-three men from Dorchester were killed in the Second World War, and are commemorated in plaques cast by Lott and Walne and added to the Memorial to the 237 men who died in the First World War. Nineteen of those who died in the Second World War were serving in the Air Force.

Thirteen

After the War

Ralph Wightman, a famous and very popular broadcaster, bravely said in 1952, during his speech on crowning the carnival queen, that Dorchester as he remembered it before the war was 'a town of rather elderly gentlemen' but now a new generation of 'relatively young' people had taken over and were getting things done. The Queen had visited Dorchester in the same year and in her speech encapsulated Dorchester's long-running problem:

I feel confident, Mr Mayor, that the Corporation of your ancient borough, while seeking to preserve the legacies of the past, will equally satisfy the needs and aspirations of the present.

The Coronation of 1953 was celebrated in traditional ways with (amongst other things) a bonfire on Poundbury, the planting of a cedar in the Borough Gardens, and a decorated shop window competition (won by Buglers with the

137 Looking up High East Street in 1948. There have only been minor changes to the buildings here, but the density of traffic has increased enormously.

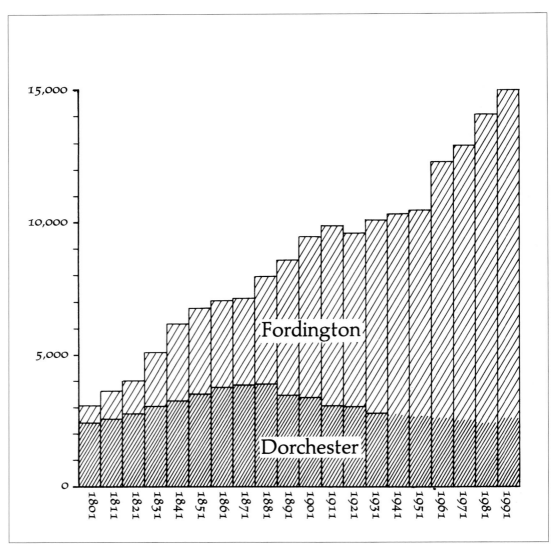

138 Dorchester's population from 1801, the first census. There was rapid growth from 1821-41, most of it in Fordington. The railway arriving in 1847 had little effect on the population, which was stable until 1871. After the enclosures of 1874, Fordington's population rises, and Dorchester's slowly declines. From 1911 to 1931 growth was slow, with an actual decrease in numbers in 1921. The 1920s *Town Guide* explains that this was because there had been 1,000 soldiers in the barracks in 1911, and none in 1921. In fact the population had grown considerably. The change in the way the census was calculated for 1951 also masks real growth to 1951. 1961 marks the start of another period of rapid growth, comparable with that of 1821-41. Dorchester and Fordington are only recorded separately up to 1931, so the separate numbers afterwards are estimates: the total is correct. From 1801-1891 church parishes were used, but after 1901 administrative areas were the basis. From 1951 the numbers are what the census calls 'in private households'. The earlier figures used include 'public households', which can make a lot of difference but cannot always be separated out. The overall total for Dorchester in 1951 was 11,622, including 553 in the barracks. From 1861 there were usually 70-100 people in the Workhouse and in the Hospital, and 50-200 in the Prison, but many of these were local people. The real problem is the barracks, where numbers fluctuate between 190 (1861) and 543 (1881). If one of the pre-1861 censuses were taken when the barracks was empty it would have a great affect on the figures. The barracks were in use from 1801. The 1941 figure is an estimate: no census was taken because of the war.

139   Maumbury Rings in July 1952, when the uncrowned Queen Elizabeth visited Dorchester. Maumbury continues to be used for open-air theatre and public occasions.

coronation regalia in spun sugar). It rained on the day, of course.

New inventions had their effect, even so. Some of the local celebrations were delayed so that people could watch the actual ceremony of coronation on the newly available television. Only very few people had a set in 1953, so, as the *Dorset County Chronicle* recorded, public (and temporary) installations were put up, and those who had sets 'threw open the doors of their homes'. At the Corn Exchange, 'thanks to the ingenuity of the television technicians of Messrs. Rogers and Dawes, nearly two hundred and fifty old people of the town' saw the 'whole of the five hour programme on 5ft by 3ft screens' set up at each end of the building. The technicians 'were on hand to deal with any emergency'. Elsewhere people crowded round the tiny contemporary sets, lucky to get a glimpse. The street parties on the following day included one

at Frome Terrace, with a maypole on the green in front of the terrace, and one in Colliton Street, where there was dancing to a piano and mouth-organ after the children had had their tea.

The emphasis was still very much on locally owned shops and businesses. The *Dorchester Through the Ages—Shopping Week August 1952* handbook claimed:

> We can show you a history second to none and today a shopping centre of high quality and great variety, with the proprietors and their staffs highly trained in the skills and mysteries of their trades.

In 1954 the town was outraged by 'a national weekly publication' (never named) which claimed that Dorchester was ten years behind the times, and that its inhabitants were mentally and physically slow. The mayor regarded it as a joke and said, 'if our lack of modern shop fronts and

140   A wintry Fordington Green in 1959. Fordington changed a lot last century around the river, but the area around the church and Green saw less alteration until recently.

"bright" displays makes us ten years behind the times, then I am quite content, for I do not want the town to lose its old and historical appearance'. The Dorchester Town Map produced in 1958 is the earliest town planning map for the area, and it claimed only printing and brewing as major industries in the town, while emphasising Dorchester's traditional and continuing importance as a shopping and market centre.

The housing report condemns a quarter of the houses in Dorchester because they are Victorian terraces, 'deficient in regard to layout, obsolete in design' and lacking modern facilities. Reluctantly the report admits that they are soundly constructed, and many could be brought up to date. This prejudice against sound and sometimes handsome houses is particularly ironic when so much later housing was both flimsy and ugly. The 1951 census had shown that 40 per cent of Dorchester's houses had no fixed bath, and this figure is a graphic demonstration of the greatest change in Dorchester since the Second World War: everyone has become more prosperous, better housed and generally better off. We may mourn the old-fashioned town of the 1950s, with its many family businesses, smaller population and apparently simpler, more cosy life, but this is pure nostalgia. When we imagine earlier times we take back with us our advances in health care, cheap food and water, education, and so on, forgetting that these are all recent things.

141 From an advertising brochure by Dorset County Stores, High East Street, early 1960s, a reminder of what grocers were like before supermarkets. By the end of the 1960s the Dorset County Stores had closed after 150 years' trading: the supermarkets had arrived.

Dorchester Barracks closed down in 1958, changing the town a good deal. There had been a barracks in Dorchester (not always in use) since the 1790s. Some of the Army land below Poundbury hill-fort was taken over for industry, and Dorchester gained its first industrial estate. Earlier businesses had developed close to the railway, but proximity to it was becoming irrelevant in the '50s. Michael Pitt-Rivers described Dorchester in 1966 in *Dorset: A Shell Guide*, as the

County town and hub, very busy but not hasty with marketing, administration and

making beer. The streets are filled with cars, country faces and country clothes, particularly on Wednesdays and Saturdays.

The Saturday Market disappeared soon afterwards, and in the later 1950s Tudor House Arcade (now leading to Waitrose) was built, followed by Georgian Arcade also in South Street; these covered shopping areas were an innovation.

Dorchester was still the market centre for a wide rural area, and was also the home of Dorset County Council. In the 1960s it still felt like a proper old-fashioned county town,

142   Parsons, High East Street, the last of the traditional grocers to close in the later 1990s. Their coffee roaster in the upper window was a Dorchester landmark because the wonderful smell stopped you in your tracks in the street. Parsons was established in 1871, taking over an earlier grocers.

with many old-established private businesses and shops.

The population expanded, with new estates at Came View and Maiden Castle and steady growth on other sides, but happily little was changed in the town centre. The Walks, too, survived, but the famous avenues of trees leading into the town were felled in the 1960s, with 150 magnificent trees in Weymouth Road being destroyed in 1969. Yellow lines marking parking restrictions arrived in the same year.

The biggest change in the 1970s was the death of the Borough. From the 14th century, local officials, and later a Mayor and Corporation, had run Dorchester, but with local government reorganisation many of their functions were taken over by West Dorset District Council.

Dorchester was lucky to avoid big development in the town centre in the post-war period, which would have meant destruction in the High Streets or South Street. The 1950s and '60s did see the demolition of a few buildings which would certainly be preserved now, such as Thurman's Art Deco fantasy, the small Georgian chapels or the Georgian theatre in Trinity Street, but generally the town did not suffer too much. Waitrose's big new shop (1984), the first large supermarket in the town, was behind the street frontages. Although there had been a few retail establishments out of the town centre, in the industrial estate for example, the greatest change to out-of-town shopping came in 1990 when Tesco built a huge supermarket right out by the bypass. Other shops there have created a second centre, and seem to have led to less business in the proper town centre.

A bypass for Dorchester was planned from the 1930s, shelved several times in the '70s, and finally built in 1987-8 at a cost of £9.2 million. Lower traffic levels in the centre made it possible to pedestrianise South Street at the same time, although traffic in the High Streets is now back up to 1987 levels. The bypass forms a new boundary to the town. There was much debate about new development within this boundary, with one site over the water meadows and another at Middle and Poundbury Farms, to the west of the town, being suggested. The latter, new farms created when Fordington Fields were enclosed in 1874, belongs to the Duchy of Cornwall.

The Prince of Wales, the owner of the Duchy, decided to use Poundbury (as the new development is called) to put into practice the ideas on architecture he expressed in his book *A Vision of Britain* (1989). Discussions on the form and nature of the development took place from 1987, and building started in 1989. The Prince has stated recently, 'If development in the

143 The fruit and vegetable stalls at Cornhill about 1955, and still surviving today on their traditional site. Background left is the Methodist chapel demolished in 1981.

144 A rush, probably after the Carnival, at the Victoria Road Fish and Chip Shop about 1960. Women wore skirts then.

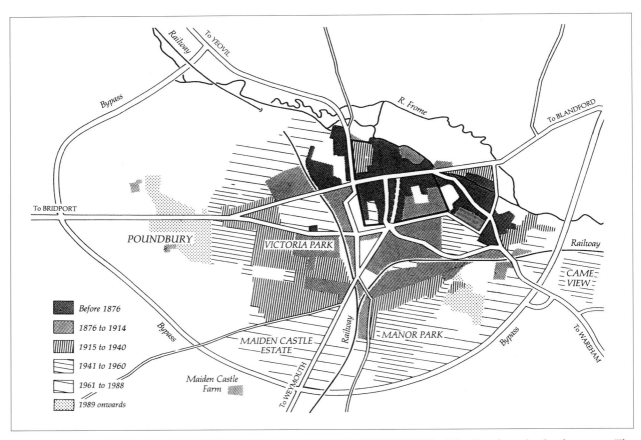

145 Dorchester's development. The medieval town inside the walls and Fordington village had expanded slightly before the enclosure of Fordington open field in 1874, The Barracks and The Grove being developed to the west of the town. The developments of 1876-1914, even those inside the town, were mostly of terraced houses, apart from the farms built further out in the open field. Fordington Farm's lands have largely disappeared under housing, and Middle Farm also. The bypass now makes the logical boundary to the town. (Map by Christopher Chaplin.)

146 The new Dorset County Library, Colliton Park, just after completion in 1966. It cost £90,000, and was the most stylish modern building in the town.

147 Dorchester West station in late December 1962, the start of the coldest winter for 200 years, when there was snow until the end of February. All the main roads were blocked but the trains continued to run.

countryside is going to take place, then I believe that it must be done in such a way as to enhance, rather than detract from, the surrounding landscape. This is what we are trying to do at Poundbury.'

Leon Crier was the master planner, and the intention was integration of workplace and home, tenanted and owner-occupied. Everything is to be within walking distance to cut down on the use of cars. In a speech in February 1999 the Prince defined his ideals for Poundbury: 'The ability to walk to a shop, to school or even to work; the provision of squares, parks and public spaces for casual encounters, children's play and relaxation; a range of house types and tenure to cater for differing circumstances and fortunes. These are the raw materials for successful urban living—essential ingredients to encourage

community growth and solidarity and, surely, to help reduce the extra costs of having to deal with the social problems that stem from not including these raw materials in the first place.' Poundbury is also experimental architecturally, using local styles for buildings set in intricate pathways and roads. Two hundred houses are now completed, and several businesses have moved in. Over the next twenty years Poundbury will add another 5,000 people to Dorchester's population (which stood at 15,041 in 1991).

Local reactions are mixed. The original proposal was for a 'new town' —impossible when Dorchester's town centre is only a mile away. The big building at the entrance to Poundbury is known locally as 'Disney Towers', and is not liked. The houses are admired, but the choice of name is not; Dorchester already had a Poundbury

148 Palace Court, Durngate Street, built on the site of the Dorchester Electric Picturedome (from 1920 the Palace Theatre) in 1984. The town has got denser since the 1960s, with many small blocks of flats, and with stables etc., being turned into offices. Fewer shopkeepers live over their shops, but there are a lot of people living in the town centre.

149 Zoned map of Dorchester showing the full Poundbury development (left). Phase One is almost complete.

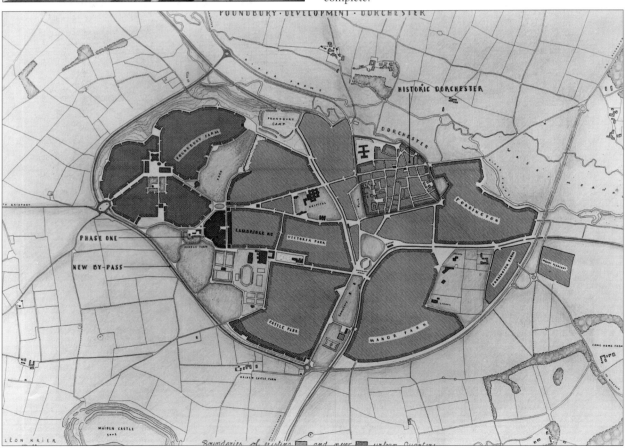

150 Brookhouse Street from Langmoor Street in the Prince of Wales's new Poundbury. The buildings are right on the street in true urban fashion.

Iron-Age hill-fort and a Poundbury Industrial Estate, neither in the same area as the new development, which is locally known as 'Princetown' or 'Charleyville' to distinguish it from the old Poundburys. It should really be called Prince's Poundbury. Will this new development become the new town centre, or will it remain a big suburb?

Claims that Dorchester is becoming like every other town, with too many chain stores and dull new buildings, surface every so often. Admittedly, locally owned shops seem to close faster than they open, and some of the new arcades seem dominated by national chains, but the essential Dorchester manages to survive. Besides, these complaints are not new. In 1907 Thomas Hardy was grumbling about change in the town: 'of the shops as I first recall them not a single one remains'. He thought Dorchester was losing its individuality and had become a London suburb. If Hardy despaired in 1907, what hope is there now?

Bibliography

Abbreviations: DCM–Dorset County Museum; DRO–Dorset Record Office; DCL–Dorset County Library; *Dorset Proceedings–Proceedings of the Dorset Natural History and Archaeological Society*; RCHM–Royal Commission on Historical Monuments; DNHAS—Dorset Natural History and Archaeological Society.

For Dorchester generally see John Hutchins, *The History and Antiquities of the County of Dorset* (first edition 1774), Dorchester pp.369-418; Fordington pp.573-7; *The Victoria County History of Dorset* Volume 2 (ed. William Page, 1908). For buildings and archaeology see RCHM *County of Dorset Volume Two South-East* (1970). *A Dorchester Camera* (1984), *Dorchester an Illustrated History* (1992) and *Dorchester* (The Archive Photographs Series) (1997), all by Jo Draper, contain many photographs. For buildings and history see David Lloyd, 'Dorchester Buildings', *Dorset Proceedings* Vol.89 (1967) pp.181-217.

Chapter 1: Earliest Times

See RCHM 1970 above and, for more recent excavations, *Maiden Castle Excavations and Field Survey 1985-6* by N.M. Sharples. English Heritage Archaeological Report no.19 (1991) also has the research on the ancient soils and land use around Dorchester. 'Maiden Castle Dorset' by R.E.M. Wheeler is in *Research Report of the Society of Antiquaries* (1943). 'Maumbury Rings, Dorchester: The Excavations of 1908-1913', by Richard Bradley, is in *Archaeologia* CV (1976), pp.2-97. *Excavations at Greyhound Yard, Dorchester 1981-4*, by Peter J. Woodward, Susan M. Davies and Alan H. Graham, is DNHAS Monograph 12 (1993). *Excavations along the Route of the Dorchester By-pass, Dorset, 1986-8*, by Roland Smith, Frances Healy, Michael Allen, Elaine Morris, I. Barnes & F.J. Woodward, is Wessex Archaeology Report no.11 (1997). 'Excavations at Coburg Road and Weymouth Road, Dorchester, 1988-9', by Roland Smith, Nick Rawlings and Ian Barnes, is in *Dorset Proceedings* 114 (1992), pp.19-46. 'Observations on the site of the "Two Barrows" Fordington Farm, Dorchester; with a note on the "Conquer Barrow" ', by Christopher Sparey-Green, is in *Dorset Proceedings* 116 (1994), pp.45-54. 'Dorchester Middle School, Coburg Road', by Phil McMahon, is in *Dorset Proceedings* 120 (1998), pp.110-11.

Chapter 2: The First Town

See RCHM 1970 for a summary of what was known up to 1970; 'Dorchester Roman Aqueduct 1998', by Bill Putnam, *Dorset Proceedings* 120 (1998), pp.94-6; 'Some Romano-British Relics found at Max Gate, Dorchester' by Thomas Hardy (1890) in *Thomas Hardy's Personal Writings* (ed. Harold Orel, 1967), pp.191-5; *Dorchester Excavations Vol.1* (1982) DNHAS Monograph 2; *Poundbury Volume 2: The Cemeteries* (1993), by D.E. Farwell and T.I. Mollison, is DNHAS Monograph 11; *Excavations at Greyhound Yard, Dorchester* (1993) by Woodward, Davies and Graham. For the closest Saxon cemetery to Dorchester see *Dorset Proceedings* 111 (p.110), 103 (p.126) and earlier volumes of that journal.

Chapter 3: Medieval Dorchester

The Municipal Records of the Borough of Dorchester, Dorset is by C.H. Mayo (1908); 'The Topography of Dorchester in the Fifteenth Century' by Jo Draper is in *Dorset Proceedings* 117 (1995), pp.21-50; for the religious houses see *The Victoria County History* (1908), pp.93-5, 101-3; *The Dorset Lay Subsidy*

Roll of 1327 (ed. Alexander R. Rumble) is Dorset Record Society publication no.6 (1980); *The Dorset Lay Subsidy Roll of 1322* (ed. A.D. Mills) is Dorset Record Society publication no.4 (1971); *The Register of John Chandler Dean of Salisbury 1404-17* (ed. T.C.B. Timmins, 1984) is in Wiltshire Record Society vol.39; *The History of Fordington* (1915) is by Richard G. Bartelot.

Chapter 4: Fires, Puritans and Revolt
See Hutchins, and RCHM 1970, and *The Municipal Records of the Borough of Dorchester* by Mayo. *Survey of Dorsetshire*, written in the 1620s by Thomas Gerard, was published by John Coker in 1732. *Fire from Heaven. Life in an English Town in the Seventeenth Century* (1992) is by David Underdown.

Chapter 5: The Georgian Town
See Hutchins; 'William Cumming M.D.', by W. Miles Barnes, *Dorset Proceedings 24* (1903), pp.34-55 has much detail of social life in Dorchester. L.C. Boswell Stone's *Memories and Traditions* (1895) is in DCM. *Elizabeth Ham by Herself* (ed. Eric Gillett, 1945) and *The Journal of Mary Frampton (1779-1846)* (ed. Harriot Georgina Mundy, 1886) give glimpses of life in the town. *The Old Roads of Dorset* (new edn., 1966), by Ronald Good, gives all the road history including turnpikes. 'The Walks and Avenues of Dorchester' (1918) by Alfred Pope is in *Dorset Proceedings*, 38, pp.22-33. The Borough Offenders Book and the All Saints settlement papers are in DRO.

Chapter 6: The Town 1800-1850
The Bath to Weymouth Line, by Colin Maggs, is Locomotion Papers no.138 (1982). *The Dorchester & Southampton Line* is by L. Tavender (Ringwood Papers, 1995). *Railways of Dorset* (1968) is by J.H. Lucking. *A short history of the Dorset County Hospital* (1902) is by John E. Acland. Directories cover the period from 1797.

Chapter 7: Casterbridge–Hardy's Town
See especially *The Mayor of Casterbridge* (1886) and *Far from the Madding Crowd* (1874). 'The Dorsetshire Labourer' (1883) was written by Hardy for *Longman's Magazine* and has been reprinted in *Thomas Hardy's Personal Writings*. Ernest Young's *Dorchester: its Ancient and Modern History* (1886) gives a detailed picture of Dorchester in the 1880s and a little earlier. *Dorset County Chronicle*; *Municipal Records of the Borough of Dorchester*; the Puddletown carrier is described in notes on Puddletown by Mrs. Legg, DCM. *William Barnes. A Life of the Dorset Poet* (1985) is by Alan Chedzoy.

Chapter 8: Late Victorian and Edwardian Dorchester
Frederick Treves, *Highways and Byways in Dorset* (1906); 'The Enclosure of Fordington Fields and the Development of Dorchester 1874-1903', by Judy Morris and Jo Draper, is in *Dorset Proceedings* 117 (1995), pp.5-14; 'The Duchy of Cornwall and the Expansion of Dorchester *c.*1900-1997', by Janet Waymark, is in *Dorset Proceedings* 119 (1997), pp.19-32; *Thomas Hardy's Brewer - the story of Eldridge, Pope & Co.* by John Seelings (nd but 1988); 'Dorchester', by Arthur Tomson, is in *Art Journal*, August 1901, pp.230-5; *A Century of Cinema in Dorset* (1996) is by Peter Dyson; *Reminiscences of Life in Dorchester 60-70 Years Ago* (1960), is by C.M. Fisher; *Views and Reviews: Dorchester* (DCL, nd but 1897/8) gives details of many town businesses. For the county in Dorchester see 'County Buildings in Dorset 1660-1830' by Christopher Chalkin in *The Georgian Group Journal*, vol.VIII, 1988, pp.56-71, and *Who's Afear'd: Dorset County Council 1889-1989* (Dorset Record Office exhibition catalogue, 1989).

Chapter 9: Victorian Legacy
For waterworks see *Reports on the Water Supply and Drainage of the Borough of Dorchester* (1854) by Arthur Whitehead (DCL); *Report to the General Board of Health … Borough of Dorchester* (1852) by Robert Rawlinson (DCM, general survey of town); Lucinda Lambton, *Temples of Convenience* (1995 edition). For Dorchester gasworks see Rawlinson (1852) and original records at DRO. See also *Dorset County Chronicle*; *Municipal Records of the Borough of Dorchester*; Proceedings against Dorchester Borough Council (Chancery Division, 16 May 1905, copy of printed transcript in DCL).

Chapter 10: First World War

Most of the information is from the *Dorset County Chronicle*. Hardy's comments are from *The Collected Letters of Thomas Hardy* vol. five 1914–1919 (edited by Richard Little Purdy and Michael Millgate, 1985). Part of an illustrated German book of *c*.1917 (in DCL) includes Dorchester POW camp. The soldier who remembered Dorchester is from 'Some Ramblings of a "Swede basher"', *Dorset Year Book*, 1959-60.

Chapter 11: Between the Wars

Dorset County Chronicle for most events; Borough Minutes (DRO); Peter Dyson, *A Century of Cinema in Dorset* (1996); 'The 1928 tourist', *Torquay Times*, 12 October 1928. For Thurman's see *A Casterbridge Ironmonger* (1993) by J.E. Skyme. For Mill Street Housing Society see *The Second Mrs Hardy* (1979) by Robert Gittings and Jo Manton, and *Letters of Emma and Florence Hardy* (Michael Millgate, 1996).

Chapter 12: Second World War

Recollections of Dorchester by Women's Institute members are in Dorset County Library. See also *Sylvia Townsend Warner's letters* (ed. William Maxwell, 1982); *The Dorset County Chronicle*; material in Dorset County Museum collected for the exhibition 'The Home Front' (1994).

Chapter 13: After the War

See *Dorset County Chronicle*; *Dorchester Town Map* 1958, with revisions 1960 and 1965, is in DCL; for Poundbury see *Duchy Review* (1999), pp.16-19; there are files of articles at DCL.

Index

References which relate to illustrations only are given in **bold**

LOCKETT's
ADDRESS TO HIS FRIENDS

AT DORCHESTER, AND ITS VICINITY.

SHOP Bills in Profe are now fo trite,
So eafy too for Folks to write,
So dull the Catalogue appears,
So grating to a Poet's Ears;
That I'm determin'd now to crofs
My little fav'rite HOBBY HORSE;
Juft take a Sip at Helicon,
Recount my WARES, and thus jog on;

FIRST then, THOMAS LOCKETT fells,
Water Colours laid on Shells,
Pencils made with Camel's Hair,
Rules for drawing laid down clear;
Books inftructive of the Art,
Every Secret will impart.
India Rubber, Paint in Drops,
Equall'd by few other Shops.
Lead of all forts, drying Oil,
Beaten Gold, and fhining Foil.
Spanifh Oker, Scarlet, Spruce,
Neatsfoot Oil for Leather Ufe.
Oil for Chamber, or your Door;
Better never fold before,
Oils that never Smoak produce,
Coarfer forts for Stable Ufe;
Iv'ry Black and Pruffian Blue,
Size of all forts, Sal'fbury Glue;
Vermillion, Rouge for Ladies fair.
Black Lead Combs for golden Hair.
Carmine, Orpiment that's red,
Yellow too, from Nature's Bed.
Verdigris and Turpentine,
Patent Blacking that will fhine,
Brown and Dutch Pink, likewife Rofe,
Drop Lake, Salts, with good Gamboge;
Verditer and Stone that's rotten,
Fuller's Earth and Spanifh Cotton;
Litmus Dutch, and Spanifh White,
Chalks to draw with, or to write;
Bronze Antique in Frofts and Spangles,
Rules for Sections or for Angles.
Gums of every kind that's good,
Ev'ry fort of Dyer's Wood.
Floor Cloths of every Size,
Ev'ry Pattern, ev'ry Price;
Colours various forts for Ufe,
LOCKETT's Warehoufe will produce.

Where you're always fure to find,
Books that will improve the Mind;
Common Prayers, fmall and large,
Uncommon ones by Squinting George.
Sermons wrote to check our Vice,
Not by Dodd, but fmooth Fordyce;
Englifh Annals, wrote by Hume,
Hiftories of Greece and Rome.
Novels for the Young and Old,
Pretty Stories, roundly told.
Shakefpear's Plays, and modern Songs,
Blackftone's Law of Rights & Wrongs,
Ev'ry Book that's wrote on Law, Sir,
All the Poets down from Chaucer.
Almanacks, and Books of Fairs,
Lifts of Commoners and Peers.
Red Books too, which partly fhew,
How it is our Millions go.

London, Sherborne, Sal'fbury News,
Politicians may perufe.
Cards for Meffages or Play,
Or that Inftruction do convey.
Mezzotinto's colour'd, plain,
Prints of Hogarth's fertile Brain.
Square and Oval Picture Frames,
Heads by Mortimer and Ames.

Should your Tenant want a Sign,
Ship, or Sloop, or Brigantine,
Lion, Bear, or Antelope,
Dunftan, Devil, or the Pope,
King's Arms, Queen's Arms, or the Head
Of ev'ry Hero, long fince dead,
Birds of Flight, and Birds of Prey,
Or Landfkips form'd in any Way,
LOCKETT's Art will foon enfure,
The Praife of every Connoiffeur.

Not to Signs alone confin'd,
Other Work employs his Mind,
Stucco, Cornice, or the Frieze,
Gilt or colour'd as you pleafe,
Wainfcot, Window Frames, or Doors,
Skirting Boards around the Floors,
(With Oil and Colours well prepar'd)
Neatly painted by the Yard.

Paper rul'd for Ladies Ufe,
Shining Ink, and Lemon Juice;
Letters ready wrote on Love,
Quills felected from the Dove;
Paper gilt or edg'd with Black,
Hambro' Quills that never crack,
Wafers of each diff'rent Hue,
German Wax, and Englifh too,
Inkftands elegant and neat,
Apparatus, quite compleat.
Made from Leather or from Wood,
Every fort in fact that's good,
LOCKETT's Warehoufe can fupply,
If the Public choofe to try.

Scented, plain, and mix'd Rappee,
Snuff in great Variety:
'Bacco too, from River James,
Other forts of various Names,
Sweet Pomatum, Eau de Luce;
Sans Parielle, and Citron Juice,
Proper for the Ladies Ufe.
Soap and Wafh Balls for the Fair,
Crefcive Compound for the Hair;
Powder Marechale and common,
For the Ladies and their Women,
Ev'ry Effence now in ufe,
All that Hybla can produce,

Cull'd by Warren's curious Eye,
LOCKETT's Warehoufe can fupply.

Books full bound, or only half,
In Morocco, Sheep, or Calf,
Marble Paper'd, green or blue,
Neatly gilt and letter'd too.

Have you need of Phyfic's Aid,
Phyfic too is LOCKETT's Trade,
Drops by Norton well prepar'd,
Pills and Drops by Doctor Ward.
Daffey's Cordial, Beaum de Vie,
Bateman's Drops and Centaury.
Hooper's, Leake's, and Stomach Pills,
Jefuit's Drops for certain Ills.
James's Powders, Drops by Norris,
Many other Med'cines for us:
Hatfield's Tincture, good for Bruifes,
Jackfon's for domeftic Ufes.
Greenough's Tincture, black and red,
Snuff Cephalic for the Head;
Herb Tobacco, Englifh Coffee,
Pills to keep the Vapours off ye.
Iffue Peas and Iffue Plaifters,
Cures in fact, for all difafters.
If by Chance the Med'cines fail
LOCKETT drives the final Nail;
Gilded Trophies he prepares,
Which the cold Coffin wears,
Crucifix for Church of Rome,
Angels for his Friends at home.

Next his Printing Room we view,
Rolling Prefs and Letter new;
Here he works his Copper-plates,
Here he prints the moiften'd Sheets;
There difpos'd in Order lie
Types by Caflon and by Fry;
Round the Room behold are hung,
Songs which fav'rite Bards have fung,
Party Squibs and Birth-Day Odes,
Epigrams, and Epifodes.
Dying Speeches, Friendly Rules,
Terms at large of Country Schools.
Lifts of Members (Votes of Credit)
How they voted---Why they did it;
Lifts of Boroughs found and true,
Names of rotten Boroughs too.

The Favors which his Friends have
fhewn
His Heart with Gratitude will own,
Determin'd ftill to perfevere,
In rendering every kind of Ware,
On Terms fufficient to enfure,
Some Orders from the Rich and Poor.

Thomas Lockett is in the 1792 Dorchester *Directory* as a printer, but his long rhyming advertisement makes it clear that he was much more than that. He must have printed this, with its pretty border.